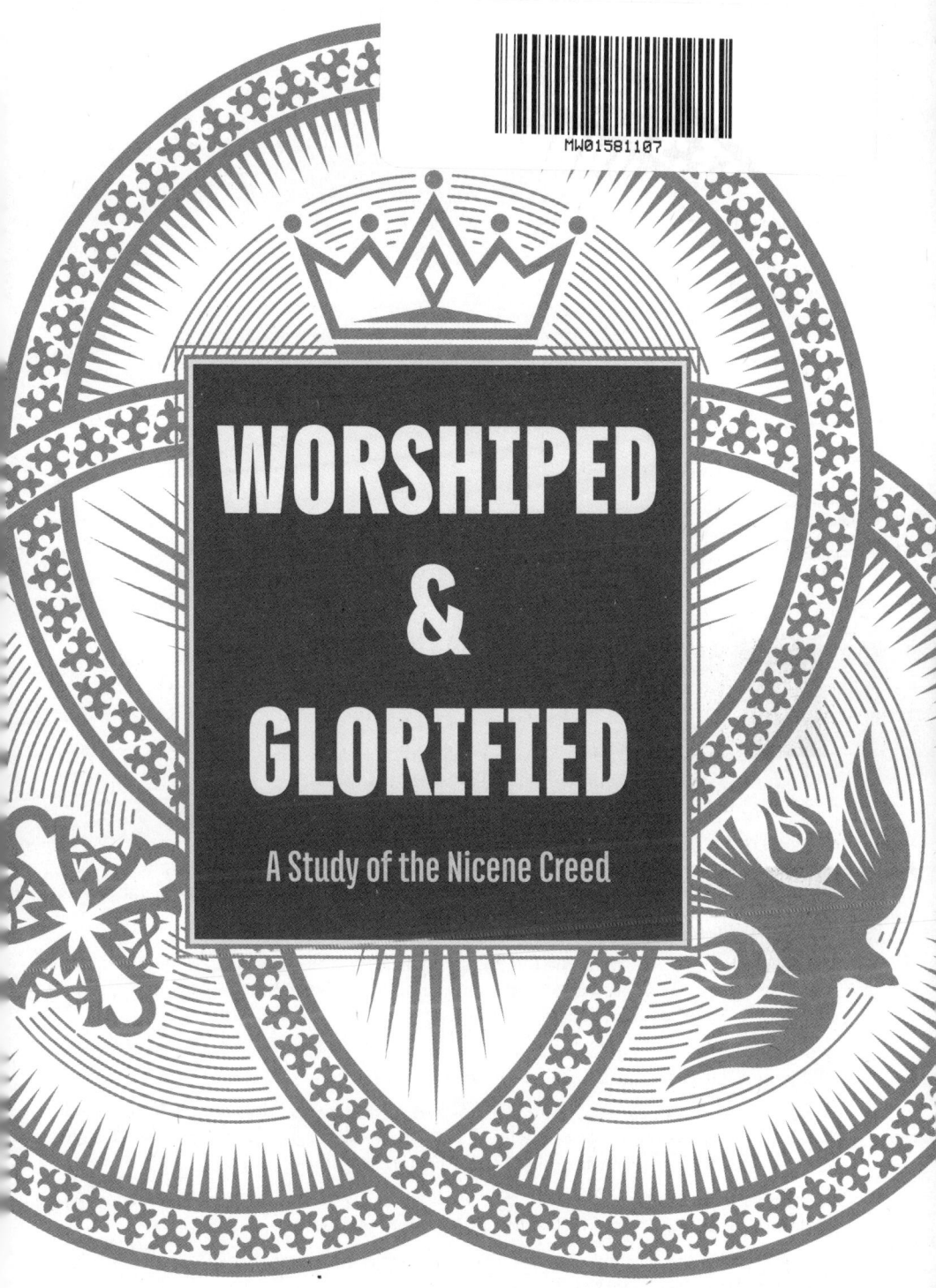

WORSHIPED & GLORIFIED

A Study of the Nicene Creed

Timothy J. Winterstein

Copyright © 2025 Concordia Publishing House
3558 S. Jefferson Ave., St. Louis, MO 63118-3968
1-800-325-3040 • cph.org

All rights reserved. No part of this publication may be reproduced, stored in a retrieval system, or transmitted, in any form or by any means, electronic, mechanical, photocopying, recording, or otherwise, without the prior written permission of Concordia Publishing House.

Written by Timothy J. Winterstein

Scripture quotations are from the ESV® Bible (The Holy Bible, English Standard Version®), copyright © 2001 by Crossway, a publishing ministry of Good News Publishers. Used by permission. All rights reserved. Italics are emphasis added by the author.

Quotations from the Small Catechism are from Luther's Small Catechism © 1986 Concordia Publishing House. All rights reserved. Italics are emphasis added by the author.

The quotations from the Lutheran Confessions in this publication are from *Concordia: The Lutheran Confessions*, second edition © 2006 Concordia Publishing House. All rights reserved. Italics are emphasis added by the author.

Quotations from *Luther's Works* in this publication are from *Luther's Works*, American Edition (82 vols.; Concordia Publishing House and Fortress Press, 1955–).

Hymn text with the abbreviation *LSB* are from *Lutheran Service Book* © 2006 Concordia Publishing House. All rights reserved.

CONTENTS

READER GUIDE

Reader Tips	5
Session 1: Why a Creed?	9
Session 2: One God	17
Session 3: One Lord	29
Session 4: For Us	45
Session 5: The Everlasting King	57
Session 6: The Lord and Giver of Life	73
Session 7: The Temple of the Holy Spirit	87
Session 8: The Story Becomes Our Story	99

LEADER GUIDE

Leader Tips	107
Session 1: Why a Creed?	111
Session 2: One God	117
Session 3: One Lord	123
Session 4: For Us	131
Session 5: The Everlasting King	137
Session 6: The Lord and Giver of Life	143
Session 7: The Temple of the Holy Spirit	149
Session 8: The Story Becomes Our Story	155

READER TIPS

Creeds (like the Nicene Creed) and confessions (like the Book of Concord) were never meant to take the place of the Scriptures. Instead, they bind us to the language and the story of the Scriptures. Each word and phrase of a confession is like a little handle connected to many interlocking pieces of the Scriptures. The words of a creed lose their usefulness when the threads between those words and the story of the Scriptures are severed. The goal of this study is to tie those threads firmly between the handles of the Nicene Creed and the many passages in the Bible to which they connect. That way, when you speak the words of the Nicene Creed with the other Christians in your congregation, you are truly *confessing*.

Confess means, literally, to "say the same thing." The original version of the Creed in Greek emphasized the corporate nature of the confession. It started with "we believe." So we *confess* with the Christians who are around us at a certain time, but there's more. We also confess with all the Christians who have gone before us and whose souls are with Christ, awaiting the resurrection. And there's more still: Over all our saying the same thing with other Christians—now, in the past, and in the future—we are *confessing* what God reveals about Himself in Jesus, as that revelation has come to us in the Scriptures. God speaks first, and then we respond in confession and praise using the words He has given to us.

The first session is a little more description heavy than the others, with the goal of laying out a little of the historical context of the production of the Creed. The middle six sessions are meant to expose the connections between the words of the Creed and the Scriptures, so that when you pull on those handles, the words of the Bible come with them. In the final session, we'll try to sum up the story the Nicene Creed tells.

In the middle of the fourth century, Cyril of Jerusalem described his teaching as framing out a house of faith, but it was up to the people hearing him to actually build the house. It is a great benefit to us as Christians to have Bibles in our homes, but only if we actually read, mark, learn, and inwardly digest the words. The Creed is a helpful outline of the story of the Bible, and knowing the outline is important so that we have a good picture of what the Holy Trinity has done to accomplish our salvation and the restoration of all things. But knowing the outline can never take the place of actually reading, hearing, and speaking the story given to us in the words of the prophets and apostles, as the Holy Spirit spoke through them. The household of God is "built on the foundation of the apostles and prophets, Christ Jesus Himself being the cornerstone, in whom the whole structure, being joined together, grows into a holy temple in the Lord" (Ephesians 2:20–21).

May God grant that this study not only give you a good grasp of the frame of the house but also drive you to continually "build the house" of your faith with the words of the Scriptures themselves. These words, of course, are not passive building blocks but are the living and active Word of God, revealed in Christ. The true Builder is the Holy Spirit, who uses those words to build us together "into a dwelling place for God" (Ephesians 2:22)! Speaking *together* God's Word; believing and worshiping *together* the God who is Father, Son, and Holy Spirit; and being built *together* by the Spirit into the temple of God in Jesus Christ—this is the holy work that happens in the church. One of the locations of that work is the Nicene Creed.

Session 1

Why a Creed?

INTRODUCTION

Why do we have creeds at all? In many churches around our country, there is no official creed confessed within the church service. The Lutheran Church has always confessed, with the wider Western Christian Church, the Apostles' Creed, the Nicene Creed, and the Athanasian Creed. It may be easy for us to take our creeds for granted, since we are so familiar with them. However, it will help us to think more deeply about them if we know how and why these creeds, especially the Nicene Creed, came to be seen and confessed as the basic summaries of the Christian faith.

SOME HISTORICAL BACKGROUND

There were many creeds in use in the first few centuries of the church. Churches often had their own local creeds, learned by those who were going to be baptized. Baptism itself often consisted of three questions along these lines: Do you believe in God the Father? Do you believe in His only Son? Do you believe in the Holy Spirit? You can see that these questions are very similar to those in our Rite of Holy Baptism and Rite of Confirmation, and they form the basic structure of the creeds we confess in our daily lives and in the Divine Service.

The Apostles' Creed is essentially the final form of those baptismal creeds, while the Nicene Creed is the final form of what was confessed after many years of controversy over the relationships between the Father, Son, and Holy Spirit. In fact, what we call the Nicene Creed is actually the elaboration of Nicaea's shorter creed by the Council of Constantinople. (But "Niceno-Constantinopolitan Creed" is harder to say!)

The controversy began in Alexandria, Egypt, around the year 318, when a presbyter (priest) named Arius challenged his bishop, Alexander, for holding that the Son was eternal with the Father. In order to bring the widening conflict to an end and have peace in the empire, Emperor Constantine called a general council in Nicaea in 325. However, the creed of Nicaea caused more disagreement, not less. The success of Nicaea was often in doubt until the Council of Constantinople in 381, called by Emperor Theodosius I. It might be easy for us to take these creeds for granted, but the controversy lasted for almost seventy-five years. This session will look more closely at some of those issues and the Scriptures that caused people to wonder about the relationship between the one God and Jesus, the Son.

UNCOVERING THE CREED

WHAT'S AT STAKE

The fourth-century controversies about the relationship between the Father and the Son were not conducted in ivory towers or decided arbitrarily by academic theologians. When Jesus appears on earth and people worship Him, there is a problem for those who believe there is only one God: How can Jesus be worshiped if He is a man? If this man is actually God in the flesh, then what about the Father? Do those who worship Jesus believe in two Gods? Those questions are the root of all the controversies, as people searched the Scriptures and came to conclusions about what the appearance of Jesus means for the one God.

No matter which side (and there were several sides) of the controversy people found themselves on in the fourth century, everyone agreed that there was one God. The question people were asking and trying to answer then is a question that we might easily ask today: How can God be one and yet three? While some of the answers given did not match the Scriptures—and even contradicted them—we should not think that any of the people were intending to be heretics. They all thought they were following the Scriptures. They all thought they were following those who had taught them Christianity. They all thought they were being faithful. So the question was really not "Is there one God?" but "How, and in what way, can God be three?" On one side, people like Arius, Eusebius of Caesarea (Maritima), Aetius, and Eunomius of Cyzicus tried in different ways to preserve the unity of God by describing the Son and the Spirit as less than the Father. They thought that if the Son, in particular, was eternal with the Father, then there would have to be two Gods, instead of one. On the other side, Athanasius, Gregory of Nazianzus, Basil of Caesarea (Cappadocia), and Gregory of Nyssa also confessed that God is one, but they wanted to emphasize in various ways the eternal, undivided unity of the three persons. The one God does not have parts but exists as Father and Son and Holy Spirit.

SCRIPTURE

> Deuteronomy 6:4–5: "Hear, O Israel: *The Lord our God, the Lord is one.* You shall love the Lord your God with all your heart and with all your soul and with all your might.

Matthew 14:31–33: "Jesus immediately reached out His hand and took hold of [Peter], saying to him, 'O you of little faith, why did you doubt?' And when they got into the boat, the wind ceased. And those in the boat worshiped Him, saying, *'Truly You are the Son of God.'*"

John 1:1–3: "In the beginning was the Word, and the Word was with God, and the Word was God. He was in the beginning with God. *All things were made through Him, and without Him was not any thing made that was made.*"

QUESTION 1: How would you briefly describe the God in whom Christians believe, as revealed in the Scriptures?

QUESTION 2: What sets Christianity apart from other monotheistic religions?

WHY THIS CONFESSION MATTERS

Just as everyone involved in the controversies of the fourth century agreed that their doctrine had to come from the Scriptures and that God was one, they also agreed that there was a fundamental difference between the Creator and the creation. However, they disagreed about whether the Son was a creature (even if the greatest and first, and even divine in some sense) or whether He was Creator. Those who, like Athanasius, confessed the Son as Creator (on the basis of passages like

John 1:3) appealed to Christian practice and worship to defend further the eternity of the Son. How could all things in creation be made through another creature? Why wouldn't the Creator simply make all things? Why would people be baptized into the name of the *Father and of the Son and of the Holy Spirit* if they were being baptized into the name of God and of His creatures? Why would Christians worship Father, Son, and Holy Spirit in the liturgy? Wouldn't they be worshiping God as well as a creature? How could a creature, even the first and best creature, save other creatures from sin and death?

All these questions helped them to clarify what the Scriptures say about God, about His creation of all things, about the Son becoming man, about God's salvation of people, and about how God gives us life. Whenever we ask about who God is, we are also asking about what God does. Throughout this study, we will ask how the confession that has come down to us over seventeen hundred years is directly related to how God restores His entire creation, including us, from the destruction of sin and death.

APPLICATION

LOOKING BACK

In the midst of controversy over the meaning of Scripture, which is often controversy over who God is, the Christians of the fourth century (and later) had to search the Scriptures. They may have used contemporary understandings of science and philosophy to back up their claims, but they wanted to know, above all, what the Scriptures revealed about God and about His salvation of human beings. When they searched the Scriptures, they summarized what they found into creeds. The word *creed* comes from the Latin word *credo*, which means "I believe." What

Christians believe is basically a summary of the story of the Scriptures, which is the story of God's salvation. Whether a church uses a formal creed or not, if they are able to summarize what the Scriptures say about God, that is their creed.

Some of their conclusions involved words that are not in the Scriptures, such as *homoousios* ("of the same being/substance"). When they were forced to defend the truth of the Son's eternal divinity with the Father and deny that any Scriptures teach that the Son had a beginning, they had to find a word that would best indicate the truth revealed in Jesus and in His Word.

WHAT THIS MEANS TODAY

Christians have always had disagreements over how to read various passages in the Scriptures. How do we come to conclusions about which interpretation is correct, or most faithful? Learning how previous Christians have come to conclusions and how they found evidence for their positions in the Scriptures reminds us that listening to the Scriptures is never finished. Even after the Council of Nicaea in 325, people argued (perhaps even more!) about who God was. Even after the Council of Constantinople in 381, people still argued and disagreed, either with the words or with the teaching itself. Even though Christians have confessed some form of the Nicene Creed for seventeen hundred years, and even though we confess the creeds as the true teaching of the Scriptures, the creeds do not automatically guarantee that people will accept those words as true. It is the Holy Spirit who gives us faith in the God to whom these words point.

The Nicene Creed does not take the place of the Scriptures, but it acts as sort of a framework that we can lay out as we read the Scriptures. It is a map to the Word of God. It is like the frame of the building, where the Scriptures and our faith in God are the building itself. In this way, the creeds act similarly to how the Small Catechism and the Book of Concord act: They bind us to the Scriptures and drive us back to them again and again, because the God whose story the creeds summarize is the God whose Scriptures testify to the Word made flesh, Jesus, whom we continue to worship and adore.

QUESTION 3: Within the Scripture passages earlier in this chapter (or others), what kind of language does the Bible give us for talking about God?

QUESTION 4: Where in our lives as Christians do we especially see the importance of the truth of God's revelation as the Trinity?

Session 2

One God

"I believe in one God,
    the Father Almighty,
        maker of heaven and earth
            and of all things visible and invisible."

INTRODUCTION

There are a lot of apparently powerful things in the world on which we depend for life. We might ask the following: How and why do rivers flood? What is the difference between crops growing and flourishing and crops dying before they're mature? Why do some people have children and others do not? In their helplessness before these created and mysterious events, humans have often searched for something or someone to put their trust in. When we have trouble understanding, we look for something that makes sense. So, we begin to speculate: Maybe the sun is a god. Or maybe there is a river god or a god of human and plant fertility. Maybe we should do something to make them happy so things will go well for us. In a world full of gods, how can you tell which is the one, true God?

The Creed, however, follows the Scriptures and concludes that if something or someone *has been made*, then it cannot be the true God. The Maker of all things must be the true God. This God is revealed as "Father" (primarily in relation to Jesus, the Son) and as the "Almighty," having all power, who has made every single thing, whether we can see it or not.

SOME HISTORICAL BACKGROUND

The controversies around the relationship between the Father and the Son were also controversies about creation. There were many theological and philosophical ideas about creation and about how everything got to be here, just as there are today. Some thought the creation was eternal. Others thought that the highest spiritual power or god would not have gotten mixed up in the physical stuff of creation, so a lesser god must have been the creator. In the fourth century, there were those like Asterius, who thought that creation would not be able to handle direct creating by God, so the Son was necessary to mediate between the Father and what He created. The Nicene Creed affirms what God reveals about Himself in the Scriptures, that the Father creates *and* that all things are created "through" the Son (John 1:3).

UNCOVERING THE CREED

"I believe in one God, the Father Almighty, . . . "

WHAT'S AT STAKE

How many Gods are there? Some people believe there are many gods. Some believe there are no gods at all. Some people speculate about what God is like, or they simply make up their own versions of God based on what they think a god should be. But Christians do not start with what *we* think about God but with what God has done, which He has revealed to us in His Word. If God is God and we are not, then we cannot simply comprehend God. We cannot "wrap our heads around" what or who God is. So He makes Himself known as God by what He says and *does*, and the God who acts in the ways recorded in the Bible is the God in whom we believe and whom we confess in the creeds.

SCRIPTURE

Isaiah 64:8–9: "But now, O Lord, You are our Father; we are the clay, and You are our potter; we are all the work of Your hand. Be not so terribly angry, O Lord, and remember not iniquity forever. Behold, please look, we are all Your people."

John 5:19–23, 26: "So Jesus said to them, 'Truly, truly, I say to you, the Son can do nothing of His own accord, but only what He sees the Father doing. For whatever the Father does, that the Son does likewise. For the Father loves the Son and shows Him all that He Himself is doing. And greater works than these will He show Him, so that you may marvel. For as the Father raises the dead and gives them life, so also the Son gives life to whom He will. The Father judges no one, but has given all judgment to the Son, that all may honor the Son, just as they honor the Father. Whoever does not honor the Son does not honor the Father who sent Him. . . . For as the Father has life in Himself, so He has granted the Son also to have life in Himself.'"

John 14:6–9: "Jesus said to [Thomas], 'I am the way, and the truth, and the life. No one comes to the Father except through Me. If you had known Me, you would have known My Father also. From now on you do know Him and have seen Him.' Philip said to Him, 'Lord, show us the Father, and it is enough for us.' Jesus said to him, 'Have I been with you so long, and you still do not know Me, Philip? Whoever has seen Me has seen the Father.'"

QUESTION 1: From these passages (or others), how do we know God as Father?

WHY THIS CONFESSION MATTERS

We want to speak as the Scriptures speak. So God is the "Almighty" or "all powerful" because the Bible describes Him that way (see Psalm 91:1 or Revelation 1:8). God is Father, not because we looked at earthly fathers and decided that God must be like them but because earthly fathers are named after God (see Ephesians 3:14–15). But we did not come to these words by thinking about what a god in general must be like and then concluding that the true God also should be like that. Instead, God gets down into the dirt of His creation, making Adam out of the earth (*adamah*). God Himself breathes life into Adam. He builds Eve from the side of Adam. Above all, we know God as all powerful and Father because the Son takes on human flesh as the Second Adam and gets down into the dirt of our sin and blood and death—from His birth, to growing in His parents' house, to His Baptism, to His suffering and death. Especially in the Gospel of John, Jesus reveals Himself as the Son, sent by the Father into our flesh and world, receiving (as man) and sending (as God) the Holy Spirit so that we would believe His Word. We know God in His revelation to us, not in our speculation about Him.

But the Father is related not only to Jesus. Now He is *our* Father! Jesus tells Mary Magdalene, "Go to My brothers and say to them, 'I am ascending to My Father and your Father, to My God and your God'" (John 20:17). Now we are among those who have "believed in His name" and have "become children of God" (John 1:12), born again from above "of water and the Spirit" (John 3:5). So also, we can pray with Jesus to "*our* Father."

"... maker of heaven and earth ..."

WHAT'S AT STAKE

Genesis 1 makes clear that God created the heavens and the earth. That is what is called a "merism," which refers not only to the two things (heaven and earth) on either end but to those two things as encompassing everything in between. We could stop there, with a general statement about God as the maker of heaven and earth and everything in between, and that would be true enough. But the Creed is not simply making a doctrinal statement we can then check off as "believed." We are saying, "I believe," and that means something not just about creation in general but about you and me as part of that creation. We are reminded by the Small Catechism that this means, "I believe that God has made *me* and all creatures" (First Article of the Apostles' Creed with meaning).

SCRIPTURE

Genesis 1:1–2: "In the beginning, God created the heavens and the earth. The earth was without form and void, and darkness was over the face of the deep. And the Spirit of God was hovering over the face of the waters."

Nehemiah 9:6: "You are the Lord, You alone. You have made

heaven, the heaven of heavens, with all their host, the earth and all that is on it, the seas and all that is in them; and You preserve all of them; and the host of heaven worships You."

Acts 17:28–29: "'In Him we live and move and have our being'; as even some of your own poets have said, 'For we are indeed His offspring.' Being then God's offspring, we ought not to think that the divine being is like gold or silver or stone, an image formed by the art and imagination of man."

QUESTION 2: What are the implications of these Scriptures (or others) with respect to how we act toward the people around us?

WHY THIS CONFESSION MATTERS

Since God has made us, we cannot escape our dependence on God. As the Small Catechism puts it, all His creating, sustaining, protecting, and providing "He does only out of fatherly, divine goodness and mercy, without any merit or worthiness in me. For all this it is my duty to thank and praise, serve and obey Him" (First Article of the Apostles' Creed with meaning). He is the Maker of all things and all people. Confessing the Nicene Creed means not only that God has made and still keeps me but that we *know and believe* that He does so. Thus, we worship God for His provision, as the rest of creation does by doing what God has designed it to do (Nehemiah 9:6). And we work for the sake of our neighbors, whom God has also made, especially as we carry out God's Law of love toward them. Since God provides for our neighbors their daily bread, through us or through others, we should do what we can to help them keep everything they need in this creation, including life, marriage, property, and reputation.

"... and of all things visible and invisible."

WHAT'S AT STAKE

Maker of *all things*, visible and invisible. There is nothing we can see, and nothing we cannot see (e.g., angels), that God has not made. This has all sorts of implications for the way we talk about creation, our bodies, sin, and redemption. It may seem obvious, but neither the devil nor sinners can make anything out of nothing the way God does. Both the devil and humans can only make use of what God has already made. Since everything is created by God, no created thing can be evil or sinful in and of itself. Instead, sin is always a distortion or an abuse of what God has made. The use of anything for sin or evil has to be distinguished from the thing itself, because God does not make evil or sin. We may abuse God's good gifts (e.g., food or drink or sexuality), but that does not make the thing itself sinful. Those are all good gifts of God for us to use according to His created purposes. When we find the evidence of sin and death in our bodies, that is not the proof that bodily existence is bad; it shows us only that creation is corrupted by sin. We should desire not to be free of our bodies or of creation itself but to be free of the sin and death that oppress God's good creation.

SCRIPTURE

John 1:1–5: "In the beginning was the Word, and the Word was with God, and the Word was God. He was in the beginning with God. All things were made through Him, and without Him was not any thing made that was made. In Him was life, and the life was the light of men. The light shines in the darkness, and the darkness has not overcome it."

Colossians 1:15–17: "[The Son] is the image of the invisible God, the firstborn of all creation. For by Him all things were created, in heaven and on earth, visible and invisible, whether thrones or dominions or rulers or authorities—all things were created through Him and for Him. And He is before all things, and in Him all things hold together."

Hebrews 11:3: "By faith we understand that the universe was created by the word of God, so that what is seen was not made out of things that are visible."

QUESTION 3: What do these Scriptures tell us about God the Father's creating related to the Son?

WHY THIS CONFESSION MATTERS

In the fourth century, no Christian disputed that God had made everything. The real question was whether the Son was part of that creation or whether He was on the side of Creator. These Scriptures clearly show us that God creates through His Word, who then took flesh within that creation. Athanasius especially makes the point that if the Son is the one by whom the Father made *all things*, then the Son is not part of what is made. The Son, then, is also to be called "Creator." Creation is the love of the Father, Son, and Holy Spirit overflowing in the making of all things, visible and invisible. And that love extends to us in Jesus, as we are remade according to Him, who is the image of the invisible God, who makes Him known to us (John 1:18).

We often count the visible, tangible things as more significant or even more real than the invisible things. But in the midst of a world where the visible things do not look like they are under God's control (and getting worse!), Paul reminds us, "So we do not lose heart. Though our outer self is wasting away, our inner self is being renewed day by day. For this light momentary affliction is preparing for us an eternal weight of glory beyond all comparison, as we look not to the things that are seen but to the things that are unseen. For the things that are seen are transient, but the things that are unseen are eternal" (2 Corinthians 4:16–18).

APPLICATION

LOOKING BACK

Creation was near the center of the controversies in the early centuries of the church's history. People had different views of what creation was and what it meant, just as they do today. They judged, as we do, based on what they could see. When they saw evil in the world, some of them were tempted to believe that the physical creation itself was evil. Some thought that physical things were less significant than spiritual things and that the goal was to escape into the spiritual realm from the lower physical realm. Some thought that God would not get too closely involved with creation, and so creation was made by a lesser God (perhaps the Son). All these ideas, and more, are still with us. We should return again and again to the Scriptures to test our ideas against the Word of God.

WHAT THIS MEANS TODAY

This First Article of the Nicene Creed sums up for us the teaching of the Scriptures about creation. People have various attitudes about our world and how we should act within and toward it. Some people come very close to making creation the god we should worship, by making environmental action the highest goal, even to the point of thinking it would be better if there were no people so that the creation could simply go its own way. Others, even among Christians, discount the worth of material things, effectively denying God's good creation of all things. They forget about the new heavens and the new earth and the resurrection of our bodies. Because sin and death have entered God's good creation, it is tempting to think that the creation itself is evil. But neither of those positions upholds God as the Father Almighty, maker of heaven and earth, and of all things visible and invisible. Instead, in Jesus, God is reconciling the world to Himself (2 Corinthians 5:19), and in the reconciliation of man and God in Jesus is the redemption of *all things* (Colossians 1:20).

We worship and give thanks to the God who has not only secured the salvation of our souls but made us, body and soul. We worship the God who has not just set up creation and let it go, like a watchmaker, but who continually upholds and sustains His creation. We worship the God who does not simply watch over things from far away but has sent His Son, through whom all things were made, into this very creation to restore it from the inside out.

QUESTION 4: What implications does this broad view of God's relationship to us and to all creation have for how we understand various controversies over human beings and the world around us? (For example, how should we treat our bodies and others' bodies? Are our bodies simply the "shell" in which our "real self" exists? Does it matter how we treat the world and live in it? Do Christians simply fall on one side or the other of the climate change controversy, or do we have a different, scripturally informed perspective?) How can we speak God's truth clearly, both to those who view the world itself as the highest goal and to those who think it will simply all be destroyed and so does not matter much?

Session 3

One Lord

"And in one Lord Jesus Christ,
   the only-begotten Son of God,
   begotten of His Father before all worlds,
   God of God, Light of Light,
   very God of very God,
   begotten, not made,
   being of one substance with the Father,
   by whom all things were made;"

INTRODUCTION

Lord is not a word most of us use outside of church. What do you think about when you hear the word *lord*? "Lords and ladies"? Someone "lording it over" someone? What do we mean, then, when we call Jesus "Lord"? What does it mean to *have* a Lord? Because when we say that we believe "in one Lord Jesus Christ," we are not simply saying that Jesus *is* Lord (which is true!). We are saying that He is *our* Lord, *my* Lord.

In the Small Catechism, Martin Luther identifies this little word *Lord* as the center of the Second Article of the Apostles' Creed. The Nicene Creed expanded that Second Article to make sure that Christians were clear about both who this Lord is and what He has done for us.

SOME HISTORICAL BACKGROUND

In the Second Article of the Nicene Creed, we get to the heart of the fourth-century controversies. Around the year 318, Alexander, Bishop of Alexandria, preached a sermon in which he said that the Son was eternal with the Father (something we probably take for granted). One of the presbyters (priests) in Alexandria was named Arius, and he objected to the confession that the Son was eternal with the Father. And from that objection grew one of the most explosive controversies in the history of the Christian Church.

The biblical words in this article were put into place at the Council of Nicaea in 325, and they were expanded slightly at the Council of Constantinople in 381. One of the specific goals at Nicaea was the condemnation of Arius and those who taught his false doctrine.

UNCOVERING THE CREED

"And in one Lord Jesus Christ, . . ."

WHAT'S AT STAKE

What does it mean to call Jesus "Lord"? Among nobility, a lord is clearly less than a king. But in the Old Testament of the Bible, the English word *Lord* is used to translate two separate Hebrew words: *Yahweh*, which is the proper name of God, and *Adonai*, which is the title "Lord." Instead of reading the proper name *Yahweh* when it appears, in Judaism, one would read *Adonai*. This was an attempt to keep people from breaking the Second Commandment and misusing God's name. (If only that was all it took!) In Greek, there is one word for "Lord": *Kyrios*. (*Kyrie* is how you would address the Lord, so we have that as the title for part of our liturgy.)

Why this word lesson? Because when the Old Testament was translated into Greek, both the name and the title for God, *Yahweh* and *Adonai*, were translated with that single word, *Kyrios*. Thus, when Jesus is called "Lord," it is not just an exalted title but a confession of and about Jesus. As Paul writes to the Corinthians, "No one can say, 'Jesus is Lord' except in the Holy Spirit" (1 Corinthians 12:3). As you read the verses below, consider what Paul is saying in 1 Corinthians 12. Is it just the ability to speak those words? Or is there something much greater at stake?

SCRIPTURE

Isaiah 6:1–3: "In the year that King Uzziah died I saw the Lord [*Adonai*] sitting upon a throne, high and lifted up; and the train of His robe filled the temple. Above Him stood the seraphim. . . . And one called to another and said: 'Holy, holy, holy is the Lord [*Yahweh*] of hosts; the whole earth is full of His glory!'"

1 Corinthians 8:5–6: "For although there may be so-called gods in heaven or on earth—as indeed there are many 'gods' and many 'lords'—yet for us there is one God, the Father, from whom are all things and for whom we exist, and one Lord, Jesus Christ, through whom are all things and through whom we exist."

John 20:27–28: "Then [Jesus] said to Thomas, 'Put your finger here, and see My hands; and put out your hand, and place it in My side. Do not disbelieve, but believe.' Thomas answered Him, 'My Lord and my God!'"

WORSHIPED & GLORIFIED: A Study of the Nicene Creed

QUESTION 1: What does it mean to say "Jesus is Lord"?

WHY THIS CONFESSION MATTERS

In this article, we are clearly speaking in the same way that the Bible speaks about Jesus: as Lord. But we should not be confused by the different words used for the Father ("one God") and for the Son ("one Lord") into thinking that the Father is called God and the Son called Lord by way of contrast with each other. It is easy to see that "God" is God, but we should also see that the Bible calls God "Lord." In the New Testament, these two words are used especially by Paul to distinguish between the Father and Jesus, His Son. This is true of the beginning of many of Paul's letters—see Romans 10:9, for example: "If you confess with your mouth that Jesus is Lord and believe in your heart that *God* raised Him from the dead, you will be saved." *Jesus is Lord* (God) and God (the Father) raised Him from the dead.

We should also be reminded that "Christ" is a title for Jesus, not a name. It means "anointed," and when the Bible speaks of Jesus being anointed, in the background is His Baptism, where the Holy Spirit descended on Him in the form of a dove and remained with Him. This, along with the voice of the Father, marked Jesus as *the* Anointed One, whom God had sent into the world. (See Acts 10:38 and Luke 4:18.)

All of this is wrapped up in just these six words: "and in one Lord Jesus Christ"!

"... the only-begotten Son of God, begotten of His Father before all worlds, ..."

WHAT'S AT STAKE

In one sense, the word *begotten* was at the very heart of the controversies in the fourth century. Three times in this article, "begotten" is used of the Son. Arius agreed that the Son was begotten, and even that He was "only-begotten." For Athanasius and the defenders of the Nicene Creed, "only-begotten" was meant to tie the Son more closely to the Father, who was "unbegotten." But Arius meant those words as a contrast. When he said that the Father was the "Unbegotten," he meant "the only eternal God," and when he said that the Son was the "only-begotten," he meant that the Son had a beginning, just as when any other father begets a son. We will see later in this session how Nicaea clarified that relationship.

The word used in the Creed and in the Scriptures below can mean "only," which is how it is used in Luke 7:12; 8:42; and 9:38. In John 1 and 3, there is an additional sense of "unique," because the Father has no Son by nature other than the Son who took on flesh. We are only sons of God by adoption through Christ, the Son.

SCRIPTURE

John 1:14, 17–18: "And the Word became flesh and dwelt among us, and we have seen His glory, glory as of the only[-begotten] Son from the Father, full of grace and truth. . . . For the law was given through Moses; grace and truth came through Jesus Christ. No one has ever seen God; the only[-begotten] God, who is at the Father's side, He has made Him known."

John 3:16–18: "For God so loved the world, that He gave His only[-begotten] Son, that whoever believes in Him should not perish but have eternal life. For God did not send His Son into the world to condemn the world, but in order that the world might be saved through Him. Whoever believes in Him is not condemned, but whoever does not believe is condemned already, because he has not believed in the name of the only[-begotten] Son of God."

QUESTION 2: Why does the Creed specify that the Son was begotten of the Father "before all worlds"?

WHY THIS CONFESSION MATTERS

Arius actually liked John 1:18, because he thought that John was making a distinction in *time* between the Father and the Son: the Father was the Unbegotten but the Son was begotten at some point—that is, the Son had a beginning. One of the questions that this argument raises is, how can we talk about God in human words? Arius saw that when the word *beget* was used of humans, it referred to a father and a son, and all of those sons had a beginning. Obviously, none of those human sons had been around exactly as long as his father!

One of the things emphasized by Athanasius, Gregory of Nyssa, and other fourth-century Nicene theologians is that we are indeed given true words to speak about God. *But* none of those words can ever say everything about the mystery of God's being. So when the Bible uses human words to describe things about the Father, the Son, and the Holy Spirit, those words are only true by *analogy*—that is, human words can never mean exactly the same thing about God as they do when applied to human beings. We have trouble speaking about God! All our words—even the words God caused to be written in the Scriptures for us—fall short of the full comprehension of God. If we could fully understand God, then we would be greater than God. So, God speaks to us, and we can confess those words as true, but we have to remember that they are all inadequate to communicate the mystery of God. And so we don't only speak or write; we worship. When we say the Creed, we're not just reciting true things about God; we are worshiping Him with the words He has given to us.

"... God of God, Light of Light, very God of very God, ..."

WHAT'S AT STAKE

These three phrases are not just repetition for the sake of repetition. All three names "God," "Light," and "very God" are used in the Bible both of the Father and of the Son. ("Very" here is not related to "a lot," as we often use it, but to the Latin word for "truth.")

Why would it be important to say the same thing about the Father and the Son? Because in the fourth century it was clearly understood that what you *called* something told you the truth about what it *was*. If certain words were used of the Father but not of the Son, then maybe the Son was not really God like the Father was God. But if the same names (Light, Wisdom, Truth, etc.) were used of both the Father and the Son, then they both must be fully divine.

There are, of course, other names for God in the Bible, but the Council of Nicaea chose these very carefully, to emphasize the equal nature of the Father and the Son.

SCRIPTURE

2 Peter 1:1: "To those who have obtained a faith of equal standing with ours by the righteousness of our God and Savior Jesus Christ."

Isaiah 60:20: "Your sun shall no more go down, nor your moon withdraw itself; for the Lord will be your everlasting light, and your days of mourning shall be ended."

John 8:12: "[Jesus said,] 'I am the light of the world. Whoever follows Me will not walk in darkness, but will have the light of life.'"

John 17:3: "And this is eternal life, that they know You, the only true God, and Jesus Christ whom You have sent."

1 John 5:20: "And we know that the Son of God has come and has given us understanding, so that we may know Him who is true; and we are in Him who is true, in His Son Jesus Christ. He is the true God and eternal life."

QUESTION 3: Can you think of other names or titles that are used of both the Father and the Son or of both the Son and the Spirit?

WHY THIS CONFESSION MATTERS

Something that might surprise us is that Arius, Eunomius, Eusebius of Nicomedia, and the rest of those who opposed Nicaea all believed that the Son was God. But their understanding of divinity was more fluid than ours. Christians who belong to the tradition that has confessed the Nicene Creed for seventeen hundred years are used to thinking of the Trinity as God and all other so-called gods (as Paul says) as not God. Arius and those who believed similarly thought that the Son could have a beginning from or in the Father and yet the Son could not be God in the way that the Father was, since there could only be one "Unbegotten," and that was the Father. Arianism said the Son and the Spirit could be God in some way but still had to be less than the Father because they came after Him.

This kind of controversy may seem far away from us, but Arius's question is still the sort of question that someone might ask of Christians: How can the Father, the Son, and the Holy Spirit all be God, and yet there are not three Gods? By reading, hearing, and meditating on the Scriptures behind the Creed's phrases and making them our own, we can better confess both what we know and what we don't know.

"... begotten, not made, being of one substance with the Father, ..."

WHAT'S AT STAKE

What is the difference between "begotten" and "made"? This phrase and the next one are the most explicit condemnations of Arius and his teaching. We confess with Nicaea that the Son is not a creature made by the Father before the rest of creation. Instead, He was "begotten before all worlds," or "before all ages" (eternally). There was never, contrary to what Arius believed, "a time when [the Son] was not."

But it is in the last part of this phrase where the fourth-century argument hits its highest pitch: "of one substance with the Father." There is a word here in Greek that was used to condemn Arius and which was a large part of the controversy after 325: *homoousios*. This is actually made up of two Greek words: *homo-* (which means "the same") and *-ousia* (which means "being/substance/essence/nature," depending on the context). It is a word that is not in the Bible, but the Council of Nicaea needed a word to describe the true nature of the Father and the Son together, and every other word they tried the Arian party was able to interpret in their own way. So they were forced to use a word that is not found in Scripture but that nonetheless says what the Scriptures say.

SCRIPTURE

> Genesis 1:1 (according to the Greek translation of the Old Testament [Septuagint]): "In the beginning, God made the heavens and the earth."

QUESTION 4: Can you think of other words that are not in the Bible but still say the same thing that the Bible says?

"... by whom all things were made;"

WHAT'S AT STAKE

This phrase, too, is directed against Arius. For him, and for later opponents of Nicaea, the Son was the Creator in some way, but He was still made by the Father in order to be the Creator. In other words, there was a blurring of the lines between Creator and creatures. Athanasius, among others, made a sharp distinction between the Creator and creatures, so that the Son was either a creature like all other creatures or He was Creator. John 1:3 was the main passage used to oppose the Arian interpretation and put the Word back with the Father as the one through whom *all things* were made. Athanasius argued that it was absurd to say both that the Son was a creature *and* that all things were made through Him. Was the Son, then, made through Himself?

SCRIPTURE

Genesis 1:3: "And God *said*, 'Let there be light,' and there was light."

John 1:1–3: "In the beginning was the Word, and the Word was with God, and the Word was God. He was in the beginning with God. All things were made through Him, and without Him was not any thing made that was made."

QUESTION 5: "The Word" in John 1 is the Greek word *Logos*, which had connotations not only of spoken words but also of reason. If Jesus is the Word made flesh, what other, richer sense can it add when we think not only of the Scriptures as the written Word of God but also of whenever God speaks and what His Word accomplishes?

WHY THIS CONFESSION MATTERS

Words can easily seem expendable or worthless. There are so many of them floating around on television, the internet, and social media. People say one thing, and then they say the opposite thing, and no one seems to notice or care. But when God speaks, He speaks His *Word*, who is the Son. The Father speaks the Word and things appear. Things happen when God speaks. The Father speaks the Word into flesh for you and for the whole world. Because Jesus is the eternal Son, things happen when He speaks too: sins are forgiven, the sick are healed, and the dead are raised. We can trust that when God speaks, not only is all creation made and sustained, but the new creation in Jesus is brought into existence. This miraculous speaking happens over and over again as unbelievers become believers! Even though we can take this miracle for granted, the Creed brings it back to our lips as we confess.

APPLICATION

LOOKING BACK

We do not have many writings of Arius himself. One of the writings we do have is a letter he wrote to Eusebius of Nicomedia, who was a former student of Arius and a friend. He writes, "What is it that we say, and think, and have taught, and teach? That the Son is not unbegotten, nor a part of the unbegotten in any way . . . but that he was constituted by [God's] will and counsel, before times and before ages, full (of grace and truth), divine, unique, unchangeable. And before he was begotten or created or ordained or founded, *he was not*. For he was not unbegotten."[1]

This brief excerpt allows us to understand a little better what Arius was trying to preserve, even if he went too far in the other direction. This is an easy trap for us to fall into. Have you ever wanted to avoid an error so much that you ended up saying something else that wasn't true? This is why we must continually return to the "pattern of the sound words" (2 Timothy 1:13) of the Scriptures, to which the creeds and the Book of Concord bind us. Also, Arius's error reminds us that our own

---

1 Edward R. Hardy, ed., *Christology of the Later Fathers*, vol. 3 of The Library of Christian Classics (Westminster Press, 1954), 330.

understanding can mislead us when we place it over the Scriptures rather than let the Scriptures lead and form our understanding.

WHAT THIS MEANS TODAY

The controversy over the nature of the Son and the relationship of the Son to the Father did not end with Nicaea in 325, nor did it end with the death of Arius in 336. And even though the church has continually confessed the Creed in this form from 381 on, the issues still remain. Islam is, in one sense, radically Arian, since it cannot conceive of the one God having a Son. That sounds to Muslims, as it did to some in the fourth century, as if we believe in more than one God. On the other hand, members of the Church of Jesus Christ of Latter-day Saints (who hold to the Book of Mormon) believe "Heavenly Father and His Son, Jesus Christ, are two separate beings but, along with the Holy Ghost (Spirit), are one in will, purpose and love."[2] That the Father and the Son were not one in being, but one in will, was one of the main points of contention from the side of Arius.

Both believing in God and talking about God are often like walking a tightrope—trying not to fall off on one side or the other. Because we cannot fully understand God, we often simply have to hold two things together at the same time. In this case, we are trying to hold together our confession that there is one God with the fact that Jesus is God, who is to be worshiped and adored. The Small Catechism puts it like this: "I believe that Jesus Christ, true God, begotten of the Father from eternity, and also true man, born of the Virgin Mary, is my Lord" (Small Catechism, Luther's explanation of the Second Article of the Creed). That sums up the conclusion drawn from the Bible by the Christians in

---

[2] "Latter-day Saints 101: What Church Members Believe," The Church of Jesus Christ of Latter-day Saints, accessed January 28, 2025, https://newsroom.churchofjesuschrist.org/article/latter-day-saints-101.

the fourth century. It may not be fully comprehensible, but that is why we say, "I *believe* . . . ," not "I *understand* . . . ."

QUESTION 6: What is the opposite of faith? Knowledge or sight? What difference does it make for how we talk about what we believe?

Session 4
For Us

"who for us men and for our salvation came
    down from heaven
and was incarnate by the Holy Spirit of the virgin Mary
and was made man;
and was crucified also for us under Pontius Pilate.
He suffered and was buried."

INTRODUCTION

As we confess this part of the Second Article of the Nicene Creed, the two key words are "for us." Consider the difference between these two sentences: "Here is a present." "Here is a present *for you*." Those two words make all the difference in the world. Consider some more sentences: "Jesus died to take away the sins of the world." "Jesus died to take away *your* sins." Or, "This is the body and blood of Jesus, given and shed." "This is the body and blood of Jesus, given and shed *for you*." Without the "for you," it's actually not good news! Here, we confess that what Jesus has done is not only a general truth or historical fact; it is an action that He accomplished *for us*.

SOME HISTORICAL BACKGROUND

These words remain roughly the same from the Council of Nicaea until today, as they passed through the councils of Constantinople (381) and Chalcedon (451). There does not seem to have been much controversy in this part of the Second Article, since everyone agreed that the Son had become incarnate and that He suffered and was buried (requiring that He actually did die).

UNCOVERING THE CREED

"who for us men and for our salvation came down from heaven…"

WHAT'S AT STAKE

In our own time, we might be tempted to get hung up on the word *men*. But the original word for "men" can be used as the general word for human beings. The emphasis in this phrase is elsewhere: "for *us* men and for *our* salvation." *We* are why Jesus "came down from heaven."

SCRIPTURE

Psalm 98:2–3: "The Lord has made known His salvation; He has revealed His righteousness in the sight of the nations. He has remembered His steadfast love and faithfulness to the house of Israel. All the ends of the earth have seen the salvation of our God."

1 Timothy 1:15: "The saying is trustworthy and deserving of

full acceptance, that Christ Jesus came into the world to save sinners, of whom I am the foremost."

Titus 3:3–7: "For we ourselves were once foolish, disobedient, led astray, slaves to various passions and pleasures, passing our days in malice and envy, hated by others and hating one another. But when the goodness and loving kindness of God our Savior appeared, He saved us, not because of works done by us in righteousness, but according to His own mercy, by the washing of regeneration and renewal of the Holy Spirit, whom He poured out on us richly through Jesus Christ our Savior, so that being justified by His grace we might become heirs according to the hope of the eternal life."

QUESTION 1: In Acts 4:12, Peter insists that "there is salvation in no one else [than Jesus], for there is no other name under heaven given among men by which we must be saved." How is this both Law and Gospel?

WHY THIS CONFESSION MATTERS

These words remind us that good news is not good news unless it is "for me." This is why the explanations of the articles of the Apostles' Creed in the Small Catechism are so profound. They emphasize continually not simply the bare historical facts of what God has done but that all of this is done for me: God has made *me*, has given *me* everything I need for this body and life, and defends *me* against danger and evil, without any merit or worthiness in *me*. This Jesus, who is both God and man, is *my* Lord; He has redeemed *me*, that I may be His own. The Holy Spirit has called *me* by the Gospel into the church and forgives all *my* sins, and He will raise up *me* and all the dead.

This is also why the summary of the Gospel in the explanation of the Lord's Supper is essential and complete: "given and shed *for you* for the forgiveness of sins." This is not only about the Sacrament of the Altar. It is the Gospel itself, full stop: Jesus' body and blood, given and shed on the cross, are for me, for the forgiveness of my sins.

> "... and was incarnate by the Holy Spirit of the virgin Mary and was made man; ..."

WHAT'S AT STAKE

What's at stake? Nothing less than the humanity of Jesus. "Incarnate" and "made man" are parallel statements, the power of this miracle belongs to the Holy Spirit, and the virgin Mary is the one from whom God chose to create a body for the Son. Before and after the fourth century, there were controversies about Jesus' human nature. They usually revolved around the seeming impossibility of one aspect or another of the miracle of the incarnation. One kind of false teaching said that Jesus only *appeared* to be fully human. After all, God wouldn't get mixed up with an actual human body, would He? A later teaching was that Mary could not truly be called the "mother of God," even though Jesus was truly God. Lutherans, with Cyril of Alexandria and the Council of Chalcedon in 451, affirm the ancient title of *Theotokos* ("God-bearer") for Mary, not for her own sake but for the sake of our confession about Jesus as God.

SCRIPTURE

Genesis 3:15: "[God said to the serpent,] 'I will put enmity between you and the woman, and between your offspring and her offspring; He shall bruise your head and you shall bruise His heel.'"

Matthew 1:21-23: "'[Mary] will bear a son, and you shall call His name Jesus, for He will save His people from their sins.' All this took place to fulfill what the Lord had spoken by the prophet: 'Behold, the virgin shall conceive and bear a son, and they shall call His name Immanuel' (which means, God with us)."

Galatians 4:4-7: "But when the fullness of time had come, God sent forth His Son, born of woman, born under the law, to redeem those who were under the law, so that we might receive adoption as sons. And because you are sons, God has sent the Spirit of His Son into our hearts, crying, 'Abba! Father!' So you are no longer a slave, but a son, and if a son, then an heir through God."

QUESTION 2: How is every true confession about Mary really a confession of Jesus?

WHY THIS CONFESSION MATTERS

This confession matters for the fullness of our salvation. In a letter (Epistle 101), Gregory of Nazianzus wrote, "For that which He has not assumed He has not healed; but that which is united to His Godhead is also saved."[3] Jesus did not only appear to have flesh; He actually had

---
3 "Letters" in *A Select Library of Nicene and Post-Nicene Fathers*, Series 2, ed. Philip Schaff and Henry Wace, vol. 7 (The Christian Literature Company, 1890; repr., Eerdmans, 1952, 1961), 440.

flesh. He did not only appear to be born from Mary; He actually was born. He had a real, human body; He died a real death; He actually rose again in His body, so that He could eat food and be touched; He still has this body, in which we will see Him when He is revealed in glory. But it is not only true for Him. Since He took on human flesh and joins us to Himself in Holy Baptism, what He did is also true for us. He assumed our flesh, so our flesh will be healed. The clearest answer to the question "What will eternal life be like?" is "whatever happened to Jesus' body will happen to ours." So we await the appearance of our "Savior, the Lord Jesus Christ, who will transform our lowly body to be like His glorious body, by the power that enables Him even to subject all things to Himself" (Philippians 3:20–21). He has united us to God, so we will be saved, body and soul.

The substance of this confession is beyond our understanding. How could the eternal Son of God take on flesh in time, from the body of a virgin? We can only worship before this mystery, which is why you may see pastors bow or kneel at this point in the Creed. You also may choose to bow your head before the mystery of God made flesh.

"… and was crucified also for us under Pontius Pilate.…"

WHAT'S AT STAKE

Besides Mary and Jesus Himself, why is Pontius Pilate the only other person to be mentioned in the Creed? Why does it not say, for example, "suffered under the Roman Empire"? Why has Pilate's name been spoken by Christians in our creeds for nearly the entire history of the church? Both the Apostles' Creed and the Nicene Creed mention his name.

Some people used to question whether Pontius Pilate was a real person. But in 1961, a stone was discovered, bearing an inscription of

"Pontius Pilate," calling him (self) the "prefect" of Judea. This phrase in the creeds identifies a particular Roman official with the history of God's salvation story. Even though people have tried to separate the story of the Bible from the history of the world, the fact is that for His own purposes, God makes use of any and all things, any and all events, any and all people. Pilate had his own desire and motivations, but God used him to bring about the salvation of the world through Jesus' crucifixion.

SCRIPTURE

Luke 23:23-25: "But [the crowds] were urgent, demanding with loud cries that He should be crucified. And their voices prevailed. So Pilate decided that their demand should be granted. He released the man who had been thrown into prison for insurrection and murder, for whom they asked, but he delivered Jesus over to their will."

Acts 4:27-28: "For truly in this city there were gathered together against Your holy servant Jesus, whom You anointed, both Herod and Pontius Pilate, along with the Gentiles and the peoples of Israel, to do whatever Your hand and Your plan had predestined to take place."

1 Timothy 6:13-16: "I charge you in the presence of God, who gives life to all things, and of Christ Jesus, who in His testimony before Pontius Pilate made the good confession, to keep the commandment unstained and free from reproach until the appearing of our Lord Jesus Christ, which He will display at the proper time—He who is the blessed and only Sovereign, the King of kings and Lord of lords, who alone has immortality, who dwells in unapproachable light, whom no one has ever seen or can see. To Him be honor and eternal dominion. Amen."

QUESTION 3: What does the mention of Pontius Pilate tell us about how God works in the world beyond what we can see?

WHY THIS CONFESSION MATTERS

Notice how the Creed connects something that happened under the authority of a specific Roman governor to our salvation: "was crucified *also for us* under Pontius Pilate." "For us," "for our salvation," "also for us." The Gospel is not an abstraction. It is embedded in the history of all creation, tied to particular events and particular people, whom God used "to do whatever [His] hand and [His] plan had predestined to take place" (Acts 4:28).

We sometimes worry about what is happening in the world: who is getting elected, how elected and appointed officials are acting, what laws are getting passed, how much in the world is contrary to what the Scriptures tell us God wants, and so on. But the greatest offense to God in the history of the world was to kill His Son. And yet in that very event (the crucifixion under Pontius Pilate, with Herod, Gentiles, and Jews—everyone—involved), God worked it all for our salvation and the salvation of the whole world. If God does so with the crucifixion of the Son whom He sent, can there be any doubt that He can work all things together for the good of those who love Him and are called according to His purpose (Romans 8:28)?

Session 4: For Us

"... He suffered and was buried."

WHAT'S AT STAKE

How did Jesus, being God, suffer? This has always been one of the questions about Jesus. Christians have confessed that God in Himself cannot suffer or die. But in the mystery of the incarnation, something that was not true of God became true: Jesus is truly God; He suffered and died; therefore, God suffered and died. It was not a fake death, to *show* us something about God or about us. It was a real death, to *do* something for us. As the following passages show, this suffering, death, and resurrection were something essential to the Son's incarnation.

SCRIPTURE

> Luke 24:26, 46–47: "[Jesus said,] 'Was it not necessary that the Christ should suffer these things and enter into His glory?' . . . 'Thus it is written, that the Christ should suffer and on the third day rise from the dead, and that repentance for the forgiveness of sins should be proclaimed in His name to all nations, beginning from Jerusalem.'"
>
> Acts 26:22–23: "[Paul said,] 'To this day I have had the help that comes from God, and so I stand here testifying both to small and great, saying nothing but what the prophets and Moses said would come to pass: that the Christ must suffer and that, by being the first to rise from the dead, He would proclaim light both to our people and to the Gentiles.'"
>
> 1 Peter 3:18: "For Christ also suffered once for sins, the righteous for the unrighteous, that He might bring us to God."

QUESTION 4: What are two things we can learn from what Jesus, Paul, and Peter say about Jesus' suffering?

WHY THIS CONFESSION MATTERS

Not only does Jesus have a real, human body, but He truly suffered. He suffered, was crucified, and was buried in a particular place at a particular time. It would take the resurrection to confirm everything that Jesus had said, but this suffering and death were not only God's will but God's will to accomplish *our salvation*.

APPLICATION

LOOKING BACK

It was probably not until the sixth century (early 500s in the East; around 589 in the West) that the Nicene Creed was recited weekly in the Divine Service. It was connected directly to the Sacrament of the Altar by the Council of Toledo in 589: "Before the Lord's Prayer is said the creed shall be chanted aloud by the congregation, testimony thereby being borne to the true faith and the people being enabled to draw near and partake of Christ's body and blood with hearts cleansed by the faith."[4]

Outside of Rome, the Creed found its place after the Gospel reading (which is where Lutherans most often have it) in the ninth century; in Rome, this placement became common in the eleventh century.[5]

---

4 J. N. D. Kelly, *Early Christian Creeds*, 3rd ed. (Longman, 1972), 351
5 Kelly, *Early Christian Creeds*, 354–57

For roughly fifteen hundred years, then, Christians have used the Creed of Nicaea (expanded at Constantinople) in the Divine Service, and for over a thousand years, they have recited it after the Gospel reading. Regardless of what other problems or corruptions there have been in the church, Christians have continually confessed the Gospel of Christ as "for us," and we will continue to do so until Jesus is revealed in glory.

WHAT THIS MEANS TODAY

Although there were those who did not believe that Jesus had a real body or that He really suffered or that He really was buried, we confess all these things. Again, this is not just about affirming historical facts (though we are doing that too). We are confessing, with the Christians of all times and places, that this is *for us*. The heart of the Gospel requires not only that these things happened, and that they be for the forgiveness of sins, but that they happened *for us* and *for our salvation*. When you say these words, emphasize "for *us*," "for *our* salvation," and "also for *us*." There is the Gospel!

QUESTION 5: Why is "for you" and "for us" so essential to the Gospel?

Session 5

The Everlasting King

"And the third day He rose again according
    to the Scriptures
  and ascended into heaven
  and sits at the right hand of the Father.
  And He will come again with glory to judge both the
    living and the dead,
whose kingdom will have no end."

INTRODUCTION

Sometimes we might wonder whether it can all really be true (yes, even Christians have doubts!). Are Jesus' words true? Are the Scriptures true? Is everything we've confessed with the Creed up to this point *true*? The only guarantee of the truth of what we confess is found here, in the end of the Second Article. Everything that Christians believe about our salvation, our life here on earth, and our resurrection hope depends on the truth of these words. As Paul says, "If Christ has not been raised, your faith is futile and you are still in your sins. . . . If in Christ we have hope in this life only, we are of all people most to be pitied" (1 Corinthians 15:17, 19). Bound up with Jesus' resurrection is His ascension, His glorification at the right hand of the Father, His coming again in glory for judgment, and His eternal kingdom.

SOME HISTORICAL BACKGROUND

One easy way to tell what controversies are addressed by this Creed is to compare it to both the Apostles' Creed and the Creed of Nicaea (prior to the expansion at Constantinople in 381). In the Apostles' Creed and the Creed of 325, this part is essentially the same—except the expanded Creed of 381 adds "whose kingdom will have no end." Why were these words so important? Between 325 and 381, there was no shortage of controversy. One of those controversies was over the teaching of a man named Marcellus, the bishop of Ancyra. He was present at the Council of Nicaea and was adamantly opposed to Arianism. However, he taught that at the end of time the Father would be the only God, because the Son would be absorbed in some way back into the Father, from whom He had come. In this way, Marcellus was trying to preserve the oneness of God against Arian accusations, but he fell into another error.

UNCOVERING THE CREED

> "And the third day He rose again according to the Scriptures . . ."

WHAT'S AT STAKE

If Jesus did not rise, both the preaching of and the believing in Jesus are "in vain," or empty and worthless (see 1 Corinthians 15:12–19). If there is no resurrection, then we believe in Jesus only for this life. But Paul says that if that were so, we should be pitied more than anyone else who lives! The resurrection sets Christianity apart from all other religions and philosophies. Apart from Jesus' resurrection (which is the power of our future resurrection, given to us now in Baptism), there is nothing particularly distinct about Christianity. Thus, *everything* is at stake.

SCRIPTURE

> Psalm 16:9–10: "Therefore my heart is glad, and my whole being rejoices; my flesh also dwells secure. For You will not abandon my soul to Sheol, or let Your holy one see corruption."
>
> Acts 2:29–31: "Brothers, I may say to you with confidence about the patriarch David that he both died and was buried, and his tomb is with us to this day. Being therefore a prophet, and knowing that God had sworn with an oath to him that He would set one of his descendants on his throne, he foresaw and spoke about the resurrection of the Christ, that He was not abandoned to Hades, nor did His flesh see corruption."
>
> 1 Corinthians 15:3–5: "For I delivered to you as of first importance what I also received: that Christ died for our sins in accordance with the Scriptures, that He was buried, that He was raised on the third day in accordance with the Scriptures, and that He appeared to Cephas, then to the twelve."

QUESTION 1: What are "the Scriptures" according to which Jesus rose from the dead?

WORSHIPED & GLORIFIED: A Study of the Nicene Creed

WHY THIS CONFESSION MATTERS

Jesus' death and resurrection belong together: If Jesus did not die, then He obviously could not be raised from the dead. If He did not rise, then He is still dead, and we are simply celebrating a long-dead teacher of an obscure Jewish sect. "But in fact Christ has been raised from the dead, the firstfruits of those who have fallen asleep" (1 Corinthians 15:20). When you are baptized, you are placed by God's Word into Jesus' death and resurrection (see Romans 6:1–11). Clothed with Christ, what happened to Him after His death will happen to you after yours. He is the "firstfruits," the first one to live a resurrection life in a human body. But we will follow Him into that life! Our physical birth can only end in physical death, but our spiritual rebirth lasts forever in the resurrection life of Jesus. This phrase is connected to the phrase in the Third Article of the Nicene Creed: "and I look for the resurrection of the dead and the life of the world to come." We are eagerly waiting for the "redemption of our bodies" (Romans 8:23). This is the hope in which we are saved, and we wait for its fulfillment with patience. In this sense, RESURRECTION is the banner that flies over our entire Christian life, from Baptism all the way to resurrection life in the new creation.

"...and ascended into heaven..."

WHAT'S AT STAKE

Ascension Day (the Thursday forty days after Easter) is not always commonly observed in our congregations, but the ascension of Jesus into heaven is essential to the life of the church until Jesus is revealed again in glory. What is at stake in confessing the ascension of Jesus? It is the confession that He is glorified in His human body and is with His church—with us—wherever we are. Jesus Himself says that if He does not ascend, the Spirit will not come (see John 16:7–11). While Jesus is present on earth with the disciples, He is present in one place at a time. But ascension is not His absence. After His ascension and glorification, He is able—because He is God, as well as man—to be present with His people at all times and in all places. This is the fulfillment of His promise in Matthew 28:20.

SCRIPTURE

> Acts 2:32–36: "This Jesus God raised up, and of that we all are witnesses. Being therefore exalted at the right hand of God, and having received from the Father the promise of the Holy Spirit, He has poured out this that you yourselves are seeing and hearing. For David did not ascend into the heavens, but he himself says, 'The Lord said to my Lord, "Sit at My right hand, until I make Your enemies Your footstool."' Let all the house of Israel therefore know for certain that God has made Him both Lord and Christ, this Jesus whom you crucified."

> Ephesians 1:18–23: "That you may know . . . what is the immeasurable greatness of His power toward us who believe, according to the working of His great might that He worked in Christ when He raised Him from the dead and seated Him at His right hand in the heavenly places, far above all rule and authority and power and dominion, and above every name that is named, not only in this age but also in the one to come. And He put all things under His feet and gave Him as head over all things to the church, which is His body, the fullness of Him who fills all in all."

> Ephesians 4:8–11: "Therefore it says, 'When He ascended on high He led a host of captives, and He gave gifts to men.' (In

saying, 'He ascended,' what does it mean but that He had also descended into the lower regions, the earth? He who descended is the one who also ascended far above all the heavens, that He might fill all things.) And He gave the apostles, the prophets, the evangelists, the shepherds and teachers."

QUESTION 2: How would you describe the importance of the ascension to someone?

WHY THIS CONFESSION MATTERS

In the mystery of God's order of salvation, no aspect is extra or superfluous. Jesus' resurrection is necessary for the hope of our resurrection, and His ascension is necessary for the continued assurance of Jesus' presence with us in His Word and Supper, as the Holy Spirit calls us to Him by the Gospel, enlightens us by His Word in preaching and Baptism, and continues to nourish us with the life of God in Jesus.

But it is more than simply a list of necessary actions. This is the outline of God's story of salvation for us in Jesus. This is the story into which we have been written by Baptism, and it is the story that continues on until we see the fullness of it in resurrection and new creation. That Kingdom, in which Jesus reigns now, is an everlasting Kingdom.

Session 5: The Everlasting King

"...and sits at the right hand of the Father...."

WHAT'S AT STAKE

This phrase may be obscure to us. Does the Father have a hand? What does it mean that Jesus "sits" at the Father's "right hand"? Sometimes our language can give us the impression that God is static, unmoving, just watching and waiting. But the "right hand" of God is anything but passive or unmoving! As we move through the following Scriptures, notice just how active is the image of God's right hand. Then, even Jesus' sitting is not some kind of relaxation but the prerequisite for God's active presence with His people.

SCRIPTURE

Exodus 15:6: "Your right hand, O Lord, glorious in power, Your right hand, O Lord, shatters the enemy."

Psalm 110:1: "The Lord says to my Lord: 'Sit at My right hand, until I make Your enemies Your footstool.'"

Romans 8:34: "Who is to condemn? Christ Jesus is the one who died—more than that, who was raised—who is at the right hand of God, who indeed is interceding for us."

1 Peter 3:21–22: "Baptism, which corresponds to this [salvation in the ark on the flood], now saves you, not as a removal of dirt from the body but as an appeal to God for a good conscience, through the resurrection of Jesus Christ, who has gone into heaven and is at the right hand of God, with angels, authorities, and powers having been subjected to Him."

QUESTION 3: From these verses or others, what activity does the right hand of God represent or include?

WHY THIS CONFESSION MATTERS

The importance of this confession of Jesus' exaltation in His resurrection, ascension, and glorification can hardly be overestimated. And once again, it comes down to the Gospel promise of Jesus for us. His suffering and death were for us. His resurrection is for us. And His continued presence with us according to His power and authority as both God and man is for us, as He intercedes for us before the Father and He continues to give us His eternal, resurrection life in Word and Sacraments. As the Solid Declaration of the Formula of Concord puts it, "He is present especially in His Church and congregation on earth as Mediator, Head, King, and High Priest. This presence is not a part, or only one half of Him. Christ's entire person is present, to which both natures belong, the divine and the human—not only according to His divinity, but also according to, and with, His received human nature. He is our Brother [Hebrews 2:17], and we are flesh of His flesh and bone of His bone [Genesis 2:23]. He has instituted His Holy Supper for the certain assurance and confirmation of this, so that He will be with us, and dwell, work, and be effective in us also according to that nature from which He has flesh and blood" (Article 8, paragraphs 78–79).

Session 5: The Everlasting King

> "… and He will come again with glory to judge both the living and the dead, …"

WHAT'S AT STAKE

The judgment, like the ascension, is not something that we talk about too much. And yet, Jesus is clear that judgment is coming and that He is the basis for that judgment. Is this a scary thing to be avoided or an occasion for rejoicing? Or maybe both? "Judging" has a bad reputation in our time, but perhaps we have not seen clearly the full scriptural witness behind these words of the Creed.

SCRIPTURE

Psalm 98:7–9: "Let the sea roar, and all that fills it; the world and those who dwell in it! Let the rivers clap their hands; let the hills sing for joy together before the LORD, for He comes to judge the earth. He will judge the world with righteousness, and the peoples with equity."

Matthew 25:31–32: "When the Son of Man comes in His glory, and all the angels with Him, then He will sit on His glorious throne. Before Him will be gathered all the nations, and He will separate people one from another as a shepherd separates the sheep from the goats."

John 3:17–19: "For God did not send His Son into the world to condemn the world, but in order that the world might be saved through Him. Whoever believes in Him is not condemned, but whoever does not believe is condemned already, because he has not believed in the name of the only Son of God. And this is the judgment: the light has come into the world, and people loved the darkness rather than the light because their works were evil."

QUESTION 4: From these passages (or others), how would you describe the judgment of God, in contrast to how most people think of God's judging?

WHY THIS CONFESSION MATTERS

We want to have a continually growing understanding of what we confess with the Creed. It is easy, in our cultural moment, to narrow the judgment of God to something that happens at the end of this world. Many people think of the judgment as God deciding whether you have done enough good to get into heaven or you have done too many bad things so He is going to send you to hell. But notice, especially in Matthew 25, that this final "judgment" is not like how judges decide cases in our judicial system. Our judges hear all the evidence and then render their judgments. But the very first thing that happens in Matthew 25 is not the hearing of evidence but the separation of those gathered before the Son of Man. The judgment is not being *decided* at this point but *rendered*.

This means that although Jesus will return in glory to deliver that judgment of the living and the dead at the end of time, that judgment essentially has already happened. "This is the judgment: the light has come into the world, and people loved the darkness rather than the light because their works were evil" (John 3:19). So the judgment that Jesus will render is based on whether people believe in Him, the Light, who has come into this dark world. You can be confident that, because He has entered this world not to condemn you but so that you might be saved through Him, you will not be condemned on the last day. This phrase, along with the rest of the Creed, is all about assuring you of the mercy of God in Jesus for you now, so that when Jesus renders the judgment, it will be in your favor because He took that condemnation on Himself at the cross.

"... whose kingdom will have no end."

WHAT'S AT STAKE

This is a clear denial of Marcellus of Ancyra's teaching that the kingdom of Jesus would come to an end when all things (including the Son) were absorbed into the Father at the end of time. Most people probably do not hold that understanding today. So what is at stake for us? To see that, we have to better understand the fullness of what Jesus' reign as king means. It is much more than a geographic area over which Jesus rules. Much like His sitting at the right hand of the Father, His kingdom is an active reigning and ruling for your sake.

SCRIPTURE

Matthew 3:1–2; 4:17: "In those days John the Baptist came preaching in the wilderness of Judea, 'Repent, for the kingdom of heaven is at hand.' . . . From that time Jesus began to preach, saying, 'Repent, for the kingdom of heaven is at hand.'"

1 Corinthians 15:24–28: "Then comes the end, when [Christ] delivers the kingdom to God the Father after destroying every rule and every authority and power. For He must reign until He has put all His enemies under His feet. The last enemy to be destroyed is death. For 'God has put all things in subjection under His feet.' But when it says, 'all things are put in subjection,' it is plain that He is excepted who put all things in subjection

under Him. When all things are subjected to Him, then the Son Himself will also be subjected to Him who put all things in subjection under Him, that God may be all in all."

Revelation 11:15: "Then the seventh angel blew his trumpet, and there were loud voices in heaven, saying, 'The kingdom of the world has become the kingdom of our Lord and of His Christ, and He shall reign forever and ever.'"

QUESTION 5: John and Jesus both say that the "kingdom of heaven is at hand" or "has come near." What are the signs that Jesus does to show that His kingdom has come on earth?

WHY THIS CONFESSION MATTERS

If we only had 1 Corinthians 15, Marcellus could be forgiven for thinking that the Son's kingdom would come to an end when the Father is "all in all" (1 Corinthians 15:28). However, Revelation 11 makes clear that Jesus, as Christ, reigns forever and ever with the Father (and the Spirit). The Trinity remains the Trinity before, during, and after the Son's incarnation. Just as important is the nature of that reign. It is not static but active, bringing health to the sick, wholeness to the demon possessed, and life to the dead. Wherever Jesus goes, bringing the words of eternal life, there is the kingdom over which He reigns. So when we pray to the Father in the Lord's Prayer, "Thy kingdom come," we pray that Jesus, the eternal King, would be present with us now and forever. It is not really a matter of whether or not the kingdom comes (Jesus has already come!), but we pray that it would come to and among us. "God's kingdom comes when our heavenly Father gives us His Holy Spirit, so that by His grace we believe His holy Word and lead godly lives here in time and there in eternity" (Small Catechism, Lord's Prayer, Second Petition).

APPLICATION

LOOKING BACK

This part of the Second Article of the Nicene Creed was expanded in 381 to exclude any idea that Jesus' reign with the Father would come to an end. The Father and the Son reign forever with the Spirit. Following the Nicene understanding of the story of God's salvation, this section narrates the exaltation of Jesus after His humiliation as God hidden in flesh and blood. As Paul says in Ephesians 4, "He who descended is the one who also ascended far above all the heavens, that He might fill all things" (v. 10).

WHAT THIS MEANS TODAY

By Baptism, you were joined to Jesus in His death and resurrection, and that will end in your resurrection, as Jesus will grant you to share in His glory. In fact, by faith we already share in that glory: "But God, being rich in mercy, because of the great love with which He loved us, even when we were dead in our trespasses, made us alive together with Christ—by grace you have been saved—*and raised us up with Him and seated us with Him in the heavenly places in Christ Jesus*, so that in the coming ages He might show the immeasurable riches of His grace in kindness toward us in Christ Jesus" (Ephesians 2:4–7). His resurrection means your resurrection; His ascension means His glory and ongoing presence with His church; and from His position at the right hand of the Father's glory, interceding for us, He will return in that glory to deliver the judgment: condemnation for those who do not believe but eternal joy and righteousness for those who believe in the one whom the Father has sent. And because Jesus' kingdom has no end, so also your sharing in the riches of that kingdom has no end. "To Him who loves us and has freed us from our sins by His blood and made us a kingdom, priests to His God and Father, to Him be glory and dominion forever and ever. Amen" (Revelation 1:5–6).

As Luther wrote in the Large Catechism, "Yes, the entire Gospel that we preach is based on this point, that we properly understand this article as that upon which our salvation and all our happiness rests. It is so rich and complete that we can never learn it fully" (Large Catechism, Part 2, paragraph 33).

QUESTION 6: How does the confession of Jesus' resurrection, ascension, glorification at the right hand of the Father and His future return in glory give us assurance and hope for our lives here and now?

Session 6
The Lord and Giver of Life

"And I believe in the Holy Spirit,
   the Lord and giver of life,
   who proceeds from the Father and the Son,
   who with the Father and the Son together is
      worshiped and glorified,
   who spoke by the prophets."

INTRODUCTION

Who is the Holy Spirit? When I was a child, the Third Article of the Nicene Creed sounded like it was a list of important things that didn't fit in the other two articles. Creation is concrete. The actions of Jesus are concrete. The First and Second Articles seem to follow the scriptural narratives closely. But when it comes to the Spirit, it almost appears to be simply a list of descriptive words or characteristics. The Third Article seems much more abstract. We will see, however, that this article, too, is a narrative of what God is doing for us, especially within the church.

SOME HISTORICAL BACKGROUND

In the original Creed of Nicaea from 325, the Third Article said only, "And [we believe] in the Holy Spirit." It was not until after the Council of Nicaea that people began to ask the same questions about the Spirit that they had asked about Jesus. Is He God? Is He God in the same way that the Father and the Son are God? What is the relationship of the Spirit with the Father and the Son? Does the Father have two Sons? Is the Spirit like a brother to Jesus? What do the Scriptures say? Not only were the same questions asked, but the questions were answered in similar ways and with similar arguments: Do we worship the Spirit? Then He must be God. Do we use the same titles for the Spirit as we do for the Son and the Father? Then He must be equally God with the Father and the Son. Do we know fully the inner workings of the relationships of the Father, Son, and Holy Spirit? No, so we must use human words, such as "proceeds," knowing they don't fully encompass the whole truth about God.

UNCOVERING THE CREED

"And I believe in the Holy Spirit, . . ."

WHAT'S AT STAKE

What is at stake is the truth of what the Scriptures say about the Holy Spirit. Clarity often comes out of controversy. In the fourth century, there were those who were called "Pneumatomachians," or those who "fight the Spirit." They generally believed that the Son was God (against Arius and others) but did not believe that the Spirit was God. He was either a creature or He came from the Son in some way. Athanasius and Basil the Great both opposed this position, and it was condemned in 381 at the

Council of Constantinople. The expansion of the Creed of Nicaea was meant to confess what the Scriptures say about the Holy Spirit.

SCRIPTURE

> Genesis 1:1–2: "In the beginning, God created the heavens and the earth. The earth was without form and void, and darkness was over the face of the deep. And the Spirit of God was hovering over the face of the waters."
>
> John 1:32–34: "And John bore witness: 'I saw the Spirit descend from heaven like a dove, and it remained on [Jesus]. I myself did not know Him, but He who sent me to baptize with water said to me, "He on whom you see the Spirit descend and remain, this is He who baptizes with the Holy Spirit." And I have seen and have borne witness that this is the Son of God.'"
>
> 1 Corinthians 2:9–10: "But, as it is written, 'What no eye has seen, nor ear heard, nor the heart of man imagined, what God has prepared for those who love Him'—these things God has revealed to us through the Spirit. For the Spirit searches everything, even the depths of God."

QUESTION 1: What in these passages (or others) shows that the Holy Spirit is a distinct person of the Trinity but neither another God nor a creature of God?

WHY THIS CONFESSION MATTERS

The Holy Spirit, with the Father and the Son, comes to us so that we will believe and be saved. The Spirit "has called *me* by the Gospel, enlightened *me* with His gifts, sanctified and kept *me* in the true faith" (Small Catechism, Creed, Third Article). When we confess, we are not speaking generically about the existence of the Holy Spirit but concretely of the work of the Spirit for our sake and on our behalf. When we say, "I believe," we are saying, "This is *for me*." And this is not a jumble of random things thrown together in the Third Article but the specific actions of the Spirit to create and grow the church by Gospel and Gifts, Word and Sacrament. This is the ongoing work of God after the ascension of Jesus. As Luke tells it, his Gospel was about "all that Jesus *began* to do and teach" (Acts 1:1), and the book of Acts is about Jesus' continued work through the Spirit: "But you will receive power when the Holy Spirit has come upon you, and you will be My witnesses in Jerusalem and in all Judea and Samaria, and to the end of the earth" (Acts 1:8). That work continues today.

"... the Lord and giver of life, ..."

WHAT'S AT STAKE

These are the first words that connect the Spirit to the same titles that are used of the Father and the Son. As we saw in the Second Article, the Christians in the fourth century confessed that the same names pointed to the same being. So the Spirit must also be God, just as the Father and the Son are God. But this confession is not just about the inner relationship of Father, Son, and Holy Spirit. It also reminds us that the Spirit is actively giving life to those who have been joined to Jesus' death and resurrection and have been restored to communion with the Father.

Session 6: The Lord and Giver of Life

SCRIPTURE

Psalm 104:27–30: "These all look to You, to give them their food in due season. When You give it to them, they gather it up; when You open Your hand, they are filled with good things. When You hide Your face, they are dismayed; when You take away their breath, they die and return to their dust. When You send forth Your Spirit, they are created, and You renew the face of the ground."

John 6:63: "It is the Spirit who gives life; the flesh is of no help at all. The words that I have spoken to you are spirit and life."

2 Corinthians 3:17–18: "Now the Lord is the Spirit, and where the Spirit of the Lord is, there is freedom. And we all, with unveiled face, beholding the glory of the Lord, are being transformed into the same image from one degree of glory to another. For this comes from the Lord who is the Spirit."

QUESTION 2: How does the Spirit give life?

WHY THIS CONFESSION MATTERS

When the Father creates and gives life by His Word (who would be made flesh), the Spirit is also present. When the Son gives life, He does so by the Spirit. When the Spirit speaks, it is the words of Jesus that He speaks, which are also the words of the Father (see John 16:12–15). Every work of God is a trinitarian work, and your salvation is the united work of Father, Son, and Holy Spirit. This is the name and life into which you were baptized (see Matthew 28:19), and it is the name by which you are blessed (see Numbers 6:22–27; 2 Corinthians 13:14). This Trinity is not only God but *your* God. The divine life that is the Father, Son, and Holy Spirit is now *your* life.

"... who proceeds from the Father and the Son, ..."

WHAT'S AT STAKE

This phrase, especially "and the Son" (which is often called the *filioque* from the Latin), is concerned with the interpretation of Jesus' words about the giving of the Holy Spirit. What is the relationship of the Spirit to the Father and the Son? The Eastern Christian Church asserts that the Spirit proceeds only from the Father, while the Western Christian Church confesses that the Spirit proceeds from both the Father and the Son. Most importantly, the procession from the Father (and the Son) is an eternal procession, like the eternal begetting of the Son from the Father, so that there was never a time when the Spirit did not exist, just as there was never a time when the Son did not exist.

SCRIPTURE

> John 15:26: "But when the Helper comes, whom I will send to you from the Father, the Spirit of truth, who proceeds from the Father, He will bear witness about Me."

> Romans 8:9: "You, however, are not in the flesh but in the Spirit, if in fact the Spirit of God dwells in you. Anyone who does not have the Spirit of Christ does not belong to Him."

> 1 Corinthians 2:12–13: "Now we have received not the spirit of the world, but the Spirit who is from God, that we might understand the things freely given us by God. And we impart

this in words not taught by human wisdom but taught by the Spirit, interpreting spiritual truths to those who are spiritual."

QUESTION 3: How would you describe the procession of the Spirit according to the above passages (or others)?

WHY THIS CONFESSION MATTERS

Paul can describe the Spirit as the "Spirit of God" and the "Spirit of Christ." However exactly it works, it is clear that the Spirit is God and that the Spirit is the one who communicates to us the Word of God, who opens our ears and minds to hear and believe, and who continually binds us to Jesus, who brings us back to the Father. Why does this matter? Because this is how someone changes from an unbeliever to a believer. How is it possible that someone can deny that Jesus is God and disbelieve one day and on the next day believe in Jesus for salvation and life? Only by the miraculous work of the Spirit, which leads to the new birth by water and the Spirit (see John 3:3–8). In God's own order of salvation, conversion to faith in the Son and the Father is impossible without the Spirit, who proceeds from the Father and the Son.

> "... who with the Father and the Son together is worshiped and glorified, ..."

WHAT'S AT STAKE

The Christian life of worship is at stake in the correct understanding of Father, Son, and Spirit. This confession is not simply abstract, theoretical speculation. Confession always turns to worship. We saw that worship of Jesus must mean that He is God, and if He is God, He is to be worshiped. So also confession of the Spirit as God means worshiping and glorifying, and worship and glory given to the Spirit mean that He must be God. There is no true confession without worship, and no true worship without confession of the one whom we worship.

This phrase can be traced to arguments in the fourth century contending that since the Spirit is named in the baptismal formula and is worshiped, then He is truly God, along with the Father and the Son. Both Athanasius and Basil the Great use language very close to what is in the Creed.

SCRIPTURE

> Matthew 28:19–20: "Go therefore and make disciples of all nations, baptizing them in the name of the Father and of the Son and of the Holy Spirit, teaching them to observe all that I have commanded you."
>
> John 3:34: "For He whom God has sent utters the words of God, for He gives the Spirit without measure."
>
> 1 Corinthians 6:19: "Or do you not know that your body is a temple of the Holy Spirit within you, whom you have from God?"

QUESTION 4: Where in the liturgies of the church do you see this worship of Father, Son, and Spirit?

WHY THIS CONFESSION MATTERS

Even though there are not as many passages about worshiping the Spirit, if we worship Jesus in true faith, this is the worship of the Holy Spirit, because to give worship and glory to the Spirit is to speak rightly of Him and His work. When the Holy Spirit is poured out on people, they testify of Jesus and what He has done, and others believe in Jesus and what He has done for them. Giving proper honor to the Spirit always means having faith in Jesus, since the Spirit will only take what is the Son's to give it to us (see John 16:14–15). The Spirit Himself glorifies Jesus, and we glorify the Spirit when we do the same. We may also pray to the Spirit (as we do in many of the hymns of Pentecost).

"... who spoke by the prophets."

WHAT'S AT STAKE

Since the late seventeenth and early eighteenth centuries, many questions have been asked about the truth and reliability of the Scriptures. Obviously, none of those questions were in view in the fourth century. What is at stake in this confession is not a particular explanation of *how* the Holy Spirit spoke through the prophets but *that* He did and that all those prophetic words were leading up to the Word of God being made flesh, conceived by the Holy Spirit, and born of the virgin Mary.

SCRIPTURE

Nehemiah 9:30: "Many years You bore with [Your people] and warned them by Your Spirit through Your prophets."

Hebrews 1:1–2: "Long ago, at many times and in many ways, God spoke to our fathers by the prophets, but in these last days He has spoken to us by His Son, whom He appointed the heir of all things, through whom also He created the world."

2 Peter 1:21: "For no prophecy was ever produced by the will of man, but men spoke from God as they were carried along by the Holy Spirit."

QUESTION 5: From these passages (or others), how would you describe the Holy Spirit speaking "by the prophets"?

WHY THIS CONFESSION MATTERS

Many, many people, and even entire church bodies, have given up the confession that the Scriptures are given to us by God. For various reasons, people pick and choose which Scriptures they will believe and which they will deny or reject. But picking and choosing when it comes to the Scriptures is like playing the game Jenga: You may be able to pull out various pieces, but eventually the tower built on the leftover pieces is going to fall. The Scriptures were certainly written by many people over many generations. So what holds them together? Only the resurrected Jesus, who says that all the Scriptures are about and testify to Him (see Luke 24 and John 5). Since the Holy Spirit is the Spirit of Jesus, and since Jesus says that the Spirit will testify of Him, we can trust that all the Scriptures, regardless of human author or time of writing, are true. These are exactly the words that the Holy Spirit wants us to have, as we hear and believe Jesus.

APPLICATION

LOOKING BACK

In the fourth century, following the Council of Nicaea, the same questions asked about the Son and His relation to the Father were asked about the Spirit. Is the Spirit God? How do we know? And, as we saw at the beginning of this session, similar answers were given. Besides the use of similar titles for the Holy Spirit as for the Father and the Son, and besides the same worship given to the Spirit as to the Father and the Son, it was also important to Athanasius, Basil, and others that we are baptized into the name of the Father and of the Son and *of the Holy Spirit*. It would be strange indeed if we were baptized into a name where only two of the three are fully God.

WHAT THIS MEANS TODAY

Sometimes the work of God in creation and redemption can seem distant to us, both in time and in space. But Baptism brings it all to bear directly on and for us. We are baptized *into* this name of the Father and of the Son and of the Holy Spirit, and so the entire trinitarian work of salvation is given to us. We are brought by the rebirth of water and the Spirit into a living connection with Jesus, who gives us the true and eternal life of the Father. In this name we are received by God and enter His presence; in this name we are given forgiveness again and again in Jesus' absolution; in this name we are blessed to live in love in the world according to our vocations. Our help is in the name of the Lord, who made heaven and earth (see Psalm 124:8)! Blessed be the name of the Lord (see Job 1:21)!

QUESTION 6: Consider Exodus 34:5–8. How is God's name more than just what He is called?

Session 7

The Temple of the Holy Spirit

"And I believe in one holy Christian and apostolic Church,
I acknowledge one Baptism for the remission of sins,
and I look for the resurrection of the dead
and the life of the world to come. Amen."

INTRODUCTION

Since you cannot see the Holy Spirit, how do you know where He is at work? What sorts of things does the Holy Spirit do? The related questions are, where is the church, and how do you know it is there? These questions have been given a lot of answers in the history of the church. What do the Scriptures say?

The Holy Spirit does what His name says: He makes holy. This part of the Creed describes how and where that "holy-making" (we usually call it "sanctification") happens, and it tells us what happens to those who are made holy (we often call them "saints").

SOME HISTORICAL BACKGROUND

Even though many of these same points of confession were in the Apostles' Creed, and most of them were not the subject of controversy, most of this article was added after 325. But the Word of God about the Spirit's work remained the same. We rejoice to confess this same Word today.

UNCOVERING THE CREED

"And I believe in one holy Christian and apostolic Church, . . ."

WHAT'S AT STAKE

One way to get at this is to ask what difference it would make if instead of saying, "I believe ...," we said, "I *see* one holy Christian and apostolic Church." If we were to define the church by what we can see rather than by what the Scriptures say, we would easily slip into false ideas of what the church is and what it should be. "I believe" is essential to this confession. Additionally, each of the adjectives attached to "Church" is essential. The church is "one," the church is "holy," the church is "Christian" (or catholic), and the church is "apostolic." We will pull on each of those threads to find the Scriptures to which they connect.

SCRIPTURE

Ephesians 2:19–22: "So then you are no longer strangers and aliens, but you are fellow citizens with the saints and members of the household of God, built on the foundation of the *apostles* and prophets, Christ Jesus Himself being the cornerstone, in whom the whole structure, being joined together, grows into a holy temple in the Lord. In Him you also are being built together into a dwelling place for God by the Spirit."

Ephesians 4:4–6: "There is *one* body and one Spirit—just as you were called to the one hope that belongs to your call—one Lord, one faith, one baptism, one God and Father of all, who is over all and through all and in all."

Ephesians 5:25–27: "Husbands, love your wives, as Christ loved the church and gave Himself up for her, that He might *sanctify* her, having cleansed her by the washing of water with the word, so that He might present the church to Himself in splendor, without spot or wrinkle or any such thing, that she might be *holy* and without blemish."

QUESTION 1: Though we put the church under the Third Article of the Creed (the Holy Spirit), how is the church a trinitarian creation?

WHY THIS CONFESSION MATTERS

In the previous lesson, we focused on "I believe" in its relation to the Holy Spirit being "for me." Here we are focusing on "I *believe*" in its relation to the difference between faith and sight. If you were to look around at the church, would *one, holy, Christian,* and *apostolic* be the adjectives you would assign? More likely, we would use adjectives such as *divided, sinful, sectarian, self-righteous,* or other similar negative words. Many people in the world would use the same, or worse, descriptors. This is why we confess that we *believe* the church, not that we see it. As the great twentieth-century German theologian Hermann Sasse put it, "The church is always an object of faith."[6] Here we confess of the church something very similar to what we confess of each baptized, believing member of the church: Though we see only sin and evil and death, we believe the promises of Christ—that we are forgiven, holy, and alive forever.

"… I acknowledge one Baptism for the remission of sins, … "

WHAT'S AT STAKE

Baptism is not just a one-time event, with no further significance, any more than physical birth is a single event, unrelated to life. Instead, it is the beginning of our life in Christ and the source of our life, since Baptism is being put into Jesus' death and resurrection. As the Large Catechism says, "So a truly Christian life is nothing other than a daily Baptism, once begun and ever to be continued" (Part 4, paragraph 65).

What does it mean that Baptism is "one"? First, it does not need to be repeated, since God's Word is never in need of correction or addition or repetition in order to work. But it is also one since we do not separate the physical element of water from the Word and the Spirit. It is one action, in which our life is begun, lived, and completed.

SCRIPTURE

John 3:3–5: "Jesus answered [Nicodemus], 'Truly, truly, I say to you, unless one is born again he cannot see the kingdom of God.' Nicodemus said to Him, 'How can a man be born when he is old? Can he enter a second time into his mother's womb and be born?' Jesus answered, 'Truly, truly, I say to you,

---

6 Norman Nagel, trans., "Article VII of the Augsburg Confession in the Present Crisis of Lutheranism" in *The Church*, vol. 3, We Confess (Concordia Publishing House, 1986), 48.

unless one is born of water and the Spirit, he cannot enter the kingdom of God.'"

Romans 6:1-5: "What shall we say then? Are we to continue in sin that grace may abound? By no means! How can we who died to sin still live in it? Do you not know that all of us who have been baptized into Christ Jesus were baptized into His death? We were buried therefore with Him by baptism into death, in order that, just as Christ was raised from the dead by the glory of the Father, we too might walk in newness of life. For if we have been united with Him in a death like His, we shall certainly be united with Him in a resurrection like His."

Ephesians 4:4-6: "There is one body and one Spirit—just as you were called to the one hope that belongs to your call—one Lord, one faith, one baptism, one God and Father of all, who is over all and through all and in all."

QUESTION 2: How is Baptism like birth and also like death?

WHY THIS CONFESSION MATTERS

If Baptism is something we do, it would be strange to confess that it is "for the remission of sins." We cannot earn or work for the forgiveness of sins because it is given freely by Jesus due to His work in His crucifixion and resurrection. But if it is not something we do, then it must be something God does. And this is why we say there is only one Baptism: When God does something, His promise is good, once and for all. We do not need to be rebaptized, because God's promise always remains for us to believe and return to it. It is also one Baptism because God does not divide the physical washing with the water from the spiritual washing with the Word by the Spirit. What God has joined together, let us not separate. There is one Baptism, the Word joined to the water, by which we are brought into the Body of Christ and joined to His death and resurrection. This is a pure gift to receive, confess, and rejoice in!

"... and I look for the resurrection of the dead ..."

WHAT'S AT STAKE

There have always been challenges to the hope of the resurrection, from both inside and outside the church. What is at stake is nothing less than the full-bodied (literally!) hope of Christians, tied to the full-bodied resurrection life of Jesus Himself.

SCRIPTURE

Ezekiel 37:13–14: "And you shall know that I am the Lord, when I open your graves, and raise you from your graves, O My people. And I will put My Spirit within you, and you shall live, and I will place you in your own land. Then you shall know that I am the Lord; I have spoken, and I will do it, declares the Lord."

Romans 1:1–4: "Paul, a servant of Christ Jesus, called to be an apostle, set apart for the gospel of God, which He promised beforehand through His prophets in the holy Scriptures, concerning His Son, who was descended from David according to the flesh and was declared to be the Son of God in power according to the Spirit of holiness by His resurrection from the dead, Jesus Christ our Lord."

Romans 8:11: "If the Spirit of Him who raised Jesus from the dead dwells in you, He who raised Christ Jesus from the dead will also give life to your mortal bodies through His Spirit who dwells in you."

QUESTION 3: How would you describe the importance of the resurrection to the Christian life?

WHY THIS CONFESSION MATTERS

We tend to disconnect the teaching of the Word of God into separate, distinct parts, but if we can keep each phrase connected not only to the Scriptures behind it but also to what comes before and after it in the Creed, we are in a better position to see the fullness of the story of God and our subplot within that story. The resurrection of the body is tied to all the pieces that we have considered so far. Follow along with the story that is told here: God makes me (and all creatures), with my body (and soul, etc.); I sin in and with my body and turn away from God toward my own desires; the eternal Son takes on a body from Mary and lives in this world, dies, and rises from the dead; He sends the Spirit from the Father, and the Spirit opens our ears, hearts, and minds to the Word of Jesus; the Spirit joins us to the one holy, catholic, and apostolic church by water and the Word, the one Baptism for the remission of sins; and as the Spirit keeps me in this church and daily and richly forgives my sins, the outcome of that baptismal, forgiving life is the resurrection of the body-and-soul person made by God, redeemed by Christ, and called into the church by the Spirit. It is all connected, and we confess here its conclusion and consummation.

"... and the life of the world to come. Amen."

WHAT'S AT STAKE

People often focus on one life or the other: Either *the next life* matters the most or *this life* matters the most. But Jesus has come to give life abundant, now *and* lasting into eternity. There is no need to pit the "now" against the "not yet." We live in Jesus here and now by faith, and we will live in Jesus in "the world to come" by sight. This is one single life, in the one and only Jesus; a life lived in the Spirit, because "to set the mind on the Spirit is life and peace" (Romans 8:6).

SCRIPTURE

Romans 8:22–25: "For we know that the whole creation has been groaning together in the pains of childbirth until now. And not only the creation, but we ourselves, who have the firstfruits of the Spirit, groan inwardly as we wait eagerly for adoption as sons, the redemption of our bodies. For in this hope we were saved. Now hope that is seen is not hope. For who hopes for what he sees? But if we hope for what we do not see, we wait for it with patience."

Titus 3:4–7: "But when the goodness and loving kindness of God our Savior appeared, He saved us, not because of works done by us in righteousness, but according to His own mercy, by the washing of regeneration and renewal of the Holy Spirit, whom He poured out on us richly through Jesus Christ our Savior, so that being justified by His grace we might become heirs according to the hope of eternal life."

1 John 5:11–12: "And this is the testimony, that God gave us eternal life, and this life is in His Son. Whoever has the Son has life; whoever does not have the Son of God does not have life."

QUESTION 4: How would you respond to someone who warns against being so heavenly minded that we are of no earthly good? Or someone who says that we should be more concerned about the good we're doing on earth than about where we go when we die? Or the person who says that we do not need to worry about creation here and now because it is all going to be destroyed?

WHY THIS CONFESSION MATTERS

These last two phrases of the Creed keep us from falling into one of two possible ditches. On the one hand, we might look around at the world and be tempted to give up, to stop loving one another according to our vocations, to stop caring for the part of the creation into which we have been put, to stop caring about the bodies God has given us—all because we are looking forward to the "life of the world to come."

On the other hand, without the hope of the resurrection of the *body* and the life of the *world* to come, we might forget that God is the maker of physical, material things. Jesus, in His own physical body, did signs like changing water into wine, feeding more than five thousand people, healing the sick, and raising the dead in their bodies. These were not just temporary placeholders for when they could be free of their bodies in God's creation. They were the effects of the resurrection of the dead and the life of the world to come reaching back into this creation, pulling it and us forward into Jesus' resurrection life. We can give up neither the hope of what is to come, when all things will be put right, nor the meaning that hope gives to all our actions here in these bodies and this world.

APPLICATION

LOOKING BACK

Baptism, resurrection, and the coming age of the new creation do not seem to have been the source of much controversy in the fourth century. The greatest point of contention in this part of the Third Article has always been over where the church is and how we recognize it. Both Arius and Athanasius, for example, claimed to be following the great and ancient tradition of the church. They both claimed that they were simply holding to what they had been taught. They both claimed to be holding to the true meaning of the Scriptures and to be representing the true church.

WHAT THIS MEANS TODAY

If the church is an article of faith, and so we cannot see it, how do we know where the church is? Jesus says that He will be with His baptized believers all the days until the completion of this age, but He is not visible to us as He was at the time He said those words to the disciples. He promised to send the Holy Spirit, but we cannot see Him either. And it gets worse when we look at the church on earth and see all the divisions, disarray, and difficulties. How can we be certain about where we find ourselves in a church made up of sinners such as we are?

Session 7: The Temple of the Holy Spirit

Even though the church is truly unseen, since we cannot see faith in people's hearts, we have not been left without "marks" by which we can see where the church is located. If you own a particular piece of property, it has a definite shape, with specific dimensions, even if you can't see it. You put a fence or boundary markers so you know where those invisible lines are. So it is with the church: Christ has marked it out for us, so we know where He is to forgive and save. "Our churches teach that one holy Church is to remain forever. The Church is the congregation of saints [Psalm 149:1] in which the Gospel is purely taught and the Sacraments are correctly administered" (Augsburg Confession, Article 7, paragraph 1).

The pure Word, the Holy Sacraments—where these are given and done and received according to Jesus' words, we can be sure that Christ's holy church will be there, and where the church is, Christ and the Spirit must be.

QUESTION 5: If you were asked how people should recognize the true church, since there are so many denominations with competing claims, how would you answer?

Session 8
The Story Becomes Our Story

INTRODUCTION

The men and women are gathered in the cool darkness of a church in Jerusalem. It is early spring in the year 351. They are standing, listening to a preacher who is seated among fragrant and flickering candles. The preacher's name is Cyril, and he is the bishop and pastor of the church in Jerusalem. Over several weeks, he has been speaking about what will happen to them on the evening when they begin their celebration of the Lord's resurrection. As they listen to the events of the Lord's death and resurrection, they follow him in the semidarkness as he moves from one place in the church to another. "Here, at this rock, He was crucified and died. And here, in this cave, He was buried, and on the third day, He rose from the dead."

SOME HISTORICAL BACKGROUND

What we call the Nicene Creed was formulated at two councils of the church, where the bishops gathered to deal with controversy and other matters that required their attention. Constantine had called the Council of Nicaea in 325 to deal, among other things, with the division in the church that Arius had begun, as well as to unify the church through unifying the bishops. In 381, Theodosius I, having become sole emperor, called the Council of Constantinople to deal with further disruptions and schisms in the church. The Creed that was finished in 381 was read aloud and recorded for us at the Council of Chalcedon in 451.

These are the historical circumstances of the compilation of the Creed we still use. It may seem as if so much (perhaps too much!) was contingent on what emperors, bishops, and other various people did. From a human perspective, it can seem as if everything in the fourth century (not to mention in all the biblical history!) depended entirely on the changes and chances of people. And yet, even while God's action may have been hidden, He was not distant or absent from any of these events. He was working in and through all these human actions to produce confessions of the scriptural faith that accurately represent the story of His creation, redemption, and sanctification.

UNCOVERING THE CREED

WHAT'S AT STAKE

In a church funded and built by Constantine the Great, Cyril of Jerusalem was able to walk with those he was teaching between the actual sites of Jesus' death and burial and resurrection. And, more importantly, when they were baptized in this church on the evening when their celebration began, he could point out to them that their Baptism joined them, by water and words and symbolic action, to the very things that Jesus did in those places for their salvation.

We aren't able to walk where Cyril and his catechumens walked (that church no longer exists as it did in Cyril's day), but our Baptism still joins us to the same realities of which he spoke: "Do you not know that all of us who have been baptized into Christ Jesus were baptized into His death? We were buried therefore with Him by baptism into death, in order that, just as Christ was raised from the dead by the glory of the Father, we too might walk in newness of life" (Romans 6:3–4).

What's at stake in our confession with the Creed of Nicaea and Constantinople is not only our faith that the events occurred but that they occurred *for us*. When we are baptized, we are written into a story that began a long time before us but which has been written for our sake and for the sake of each and every person whom God brings into existence.

SCRIPTURE

> Romans 4:23–25: "But the words 'it was counted to [Abraham]' were not written for his sake alone, but for ours also. It will be counted to us who believe in Him who raised from the dead Jesus our Lord, who was delivered up for our trespasses and raised for our justification."

> 1 Corinthians 10:11: "Now these things happened to them as an example, but they were written down for our instruction, on whom the end of the ages has come."

QUESTION 1: Whose story is primary, ours or God's? If asked, Christians will likely say God's, but how does that work out in practice in our lives? What difference does it make for your life if you think of the Bible's story as the story into which you are written at Baptism rather than thinking of your story as the main story into which God and the Bible have to fit?

WHY THIS CONFESSION MATTERS

One piece of advice I have heard, and which we have tried to pass on to our children, is this: Tell yourself a different story. When we are anxious or depressed, when we feel like nothing is going right, or when we have faced overwhelming criticism, we start to believe that those words tell us the only story that matters. In our world, people often feel pressured (by the culture, by social media, by internal pressure) to make and remake themselves until they feel like they are finally their "true" selves. Christians have the comfort and assurance that the identity given to us in Christ is absolute and unconditional, no matter what we or anyone else says. More than simply trying to tell ourselves a different story, God tells us a story in Christ that does not depend on what we have done or left undone or on what other stories are told about us. The Creed gives us a story into which we are baptized and to which we can turn when all the other stories fail to give us peace.

APPLICATION

LOOKING BACK

As we have considered some of the controversies of the fourth century around creation, around the Son and the Holy Spirit, and around the Holy Trinity, the main question has always been this: What do the Scriptures say? We have seen, however, that what was clear to one person in the Scriptures was not clear at all to another. To Arius, it was clear that the Son had to have a beginning because He was a *Son* and not the Father. But to Athanasius, it was equally as clear that *this* Father and Son, being God, were different from a human father with a human son. To Arius, the story of the Scriptures was that the Son was created, did His work, and was exalted by the Father to a higher position (from a lower position to a higher one). To Athanasius, the story of the Scriptures was that the Son was eternally exalted but then lowered Himself to share, in flesh, our human existence, taking our sin on Himself, dying, rising from the dead, and being exalted again in His flesh to the right hand of God's power (from the highest position, to the lowest position, to the highest again). These two different stories meant that they saw everything in the Scriptures differently.

WHAT THIS MEANS TODAY

As Solomon says, "There is nothing new under the sun" (Ecclesiastes 1:9). Whether it is the specific false teachings that arise again and again or the way that God's truth fares in the world, or the way that people go about controversies in the church or the perennial questions about the Trinity, what we learn about the fourth century (or the eleventh century or the sixteenth . . .) helps us not only to see how people dealt with questions concerning what they believed and confessed but to think more deeply about what we believe and confess. What are we actually doing when we say a creed each Lord's Day? What does it mean to say *this* creed? As with anything we do often—and especially things we do in the church—it is important to be renewed and refreshed in our knowledge and faith so that the words of our creeds and confessions would bring up to the surface the Scriptures to which they are tied, and to which they tie us.

What we learn from the fourth-century controversies is that we are tied not only to particular words or verses but to the entire story told by these words, verses, chapters, and books. Because we are baptized into the name of the God—Father, Son, and Holy Spirit—whose story this is, we are brought into the very story we confess each week. This is now *our* story, and everything we confess in our words and actions tells the story of what God has done for us.

QUESTION 2: How would you explain to someone why we continue to use these ancient words each Sunday?

LEADER TIPS

Whenever I am instructing someone in the Christian faith, especially those who are joining a congregation I am serving as pastor, I say that if I tell them anything about Christianity, about what we believe or about what we do, then I ought to be able to give them Scripture on which it is based. If not, I cannot expect them to believe it. My goal in this study is to expose the biblical foundation on which the Nicene Creed rests, so that the faith of those who confess the Creed will be firmly established in the Word of God, which testifies to our Lord Jesus Christ.

As the leader, your primary job is to refer people continually to those Scriptures. But there are some secondary tasks that can add some texture to their knowledge of the Word. One of those is to know a little about the historical context in which the Nicene Creed ("finished" in 381 at the Council of Constantinople) came to be. If you are not already familiar with some of the major players in the fourth century, you might do an internet search for Arius, Alexander of Alexandria, Athanasius of Alexandria, Eusebius of Caesarea, Eusebius of Nicomedia, Asterius, Basil of Caesarea (a different Caesarea from Eusebius!), Gregory of Nazianzus, and Gregory of Nyssa. You might also want to be familiar with the order of emperors, who often had much to do with the councils. Constantine the Great as well as his three sons (Constantine II, Constantius, and Constans) were important in shaping who was heard and when. Valens and Julian (called "the Apostate" because he rejected Christianity for paganism) were influential in smaller ways. Theodosius I is important for supporting the confession of Nicaea and calling the Council of Constantinople.

For broad outlines of what we confess about the Holy Trinity, Luther's explanations of the Apostles' Creed in the Small and Large Catechisms are indispensable. You could also consult a general history, such as J. N. D. Kelly's *Early Christian Creeds*. For the primary sources themselves, including the records of the councils, you can read many of them for free online at the Christian Classics Ethereal Library (ccel.org/fathers).

Leader Guide for Session 1
Why a Creed?

KEY TAKEAWAYS

The main thing here is to try to move past the very easy temptation to take the Creed for granted as we speak it. It is easy to say the Nicene Creed (or any creed) week after week and forget that its statements are tied directly to particular Bible passages and that they were forged in the heat of intense debate about what those Scriptures actually mean. We should also see that both the scriptural truth and the anti-scriptural error, which seem clear to us, were not always clear in the fourth century. No one was trying to be a heretic; everyone was trying to work out how God could be both one and three, in light of Jesus. To this end, the Scriptures in this session are trying to set up the "problem": Everyone believed there was only one God, but then Jesus appears and He is worshiped. How can people worship Jesus and His Father without there being two (or later, with the Holy Spirit, three) Gods?

OPENING PRAYER

O Lord God, our heavenly Father, You have revealed Your great love in Jesus, the eternal Son in flesh. Give us true and living faith in Him by Your Holy Spirit and keep us in Your love so that we have the assurance that we are reconciled with You forever; through Jesus Christ, Your Son, our Lord, who lives and reigns with You and the Holy Spirit, one God, now and forever. Amen.

Hymn: "Triune God, Be Thou Our Stay" (*Lutheran Service Book* 505)

QUESTION 1: How would you briefly describe the God in whom Christians believe, as revealed in the Scriptures?

ANSWER 1: We should not be content to speak simply of "God," since many people use that word but do not mean the God of the Scriptures. In the appearance of Jesus, who speaks of His Father, who sent Him, and the Spirit, whom He will send from the Father, God is revealed to us to be Father, Son, and Holy Spirit.

QUESTION 2: What sets Christianity apart from other monotheistic religions?

ANSWER 2: We often hear about so-called monotheistic religions, a description that people use to distinguish religions like Hinduism from Judaism, Christianity, and Islam. The main point here, under the Scripture passages, is that Christians are bound by God's revelation of Himself and not presuppositions about monotheism.

QUESTION 3: Within the Scripture passages earlier in this chapter (or others), what kind of language does the Bible give us for talking about God?

ANSWER 3: The emphasis is on Jesus speaking of His Father and of the Spirit, whom He will send from the Father. One good place to look is John 16:12–14.

QUESTION 4: Where in our lives as Christians do we especially see the importance of the truth of God's revelation as the Trinity?

ANSWER 4: Because Baptism is the beginning and ongoing reality of our life in Christ, and Baptism is in the (singular) name of the Father, Son, and Holy Spirit, Titus 3:4–7 may be helpful.

FOR FURTHER INVESTIGATION

Martin Chemnitz, *The Two Natures in Christ*, trans. J. A. O. Preus, Chemnitz's Works, vol. 6 (Concordia Publishing House, 1971).

ADDITIONAL INFORMATION

The creeds have not always been used in the same way as we use them now (typically, the Apostles' Creed in the Rite of Holy Baptism, in catechesis, and in private prayer; the Nicene Creed when we gather as the church to receive the body and blood of Jesus in the Divine Service). But however they are used, they are meant to guide us as we read the Scriptures. Two images that might help us see this are *outline* and *map*. If we have an outline to a novel or an essay, we may have not yet written or read the novel or essay itself. The outline (if it is a good one!) shows us the structure of the full work. The creeds are meant to show us the structure of the scriptural story of God's salvation. If we have a map in front of us, we might be able to say we "know" the location of various places and their relative relationships to each other. But we do not actually *know* the places until we have traveled there on the roads and seen the sights marked on the map. Then what was only two-dimensional—however accurate and true—becomes for us three-dimensional as we encounter the living reality. In a similar way, the creeds are the map to the Scriptures, which describe the reality of the living God, who has also brought us into His story, in His world.

BONUS QUESTIONS

1. Besides God's revelation in the Scriptures and the summary in the Creed of what we believe, the rubber really hits the road in how we worship and how we talk about God. How so?

2. Where do we see the Trinity in the liturgy? How are those instances often connected to Baptism, which is our primary encounter with the Trinity?

3. How might thinking clearly and explicitly about God as Trinity, and worshiping this God, cause us to think differently about God-talk that we encounter in the world? Examples might include singing "God Bless America" at a baseball game, the phrase "In God We Trust" on our currency, "one nation under God" in the Pledge of Allegiance, and discussion around the United States as a so-called Christian nation.

Leader Guide for Session 2
One God

KEY TAKEAWAYS

When the Scriptures talk about Yahweh (usually translated "the Lord" in the Old Testament) as the one, true God, this is often connected to the fact that He alone made all things. God is Father both in relation to the Son and through Jesus in relation to us. John 1 and 3 and the Lord's Prayer (Matthew 6:9–15; Luke 11:1–4) are important here. We know God not by speculation about what gods in general are like but by how He has revealed Himself to us. God has revealed Himself as Creator of all things, and we confess that He is our Creator.

OPENING PRAYER

O Almighty God and Father, You created all things through Your Word, giving us life by Your Spirit. As You have remade us by water and the Spirit according to Your true image in Jesus, keep us always as Your dear children, so that we may forever thank and praise, serve and obey You;

through Jesus Christ, Your Son, our Lord, who lives and reigns with You and the Holy Spirit, one God, now and forever. Amen.

Hymn: "We Praise You and Acknowledge You, O God" (*Lutheran Service Book* 941)

QUESTION 1: From these passages (or others), how do we know God as Father?

ANSWER 1: The emphasis is on Jesus revealing the Father to us.

QUESTION 2: What are the implications of these Scriptures (or others) with respect to how we act toward the people around us?

ANSWER 2: The fact that God created all people reminds us that they, too, were created to worship the true God. But the Bible doesn't stop there. If they were created by God, then they are also the objects of the Father's saving love in the Son. In Athens, Paul doesn't stop with God's creation but drives on to the redemption of God's creation in the death and resurrection of Jesus.

QUESTION 3: What do these Scriptures tell us about God the Father's creating related to the Son?

ANSWER 3: The Scriptures emphasize the Father creating through the Son.

QUESTION 4: What implications does this broad view of God's relationship to us and to all creation have for how we understand various controversies over human beings and the world around us? (For example, how should we treat our bodies and others' bodies? Are our bodies simply the "shell" in which our "real self" exists? Does it matter how we treat the world and live in it? Do Christians simply fall on one side or the other of the climate change controversy, or do we have a different, scripturally informed perspective?) How can we speak God's truth clearly, both to those who view the world itself as the highest goal and to those who think it will simply all be destroyed and so does not matter much?

ANSWER 4: If all things are God's creation, then we do not have the "right" to do what we want—with our own bodies, with other humans' bodies, or with creation as a whole. The bodies He has given us are not temporary shells that do not matter but are part of the very existence of our created humanity. The creation will not simply be destroyed, but it will be remade in a renewed, complete, perfect form (purified from sin and death). If our bodies are going to be raised, it matters what we do with them. If the creation is going to be renewed, it matters how we live in it.

FOR FURTHER INVESTIGATION

Valerius Herberger, *The Great Works of God: Parts One and Two*, trans. Matthew Carver (Concordia Publishing House, 2010), especially pages 1–124.

Martin Chemnitz, *The Lord's Prayer*, trans. Georg Williams, Chemnitz's Works, vol. 5 (Concordia Publishing House, 2007), especially chapter 2.

ADDITIONAL INFORMATION

In the fourth-century controversies over the relationship between the Father and the Son, creation was a key part of the question. Arius, Eunomius, and others put the Son on the creation side, while Athanasius, Basil, and others confessed that all things were made through the Son and, therefore, the Son must be Creator with the Father.

BONUS QUESTIONS

1. One of the major emphases here is that we know God by His specific, concrete activity and not, first of all, by general characteristics.

2. We believe God created all things, including human beings, to be "very good" (Genesis 1:31). The article on creation raises questions in relation to how the creation is now—corrupted by sin and death. Because of sin, when we look at the creation, what can we know about God? Do we know whether God is for us or against us? When we see the majesty of mountains or oceans, we might say we do. But what about when that ocean turns into a tsunami or the mountain is a volcano that erupts and brings destruction? Here it may be helpful to connect the dots from creation as it was and creation as it is under sin and death to Jesus in His body and to the new creation.

Leader Guide for Session 3
One Lord

KEY TAKEAWAYS

If we remember from the previous session that "Yahweh" is translated into English as "Lord" in the Old Testament, this gets us a little closer to the importance of calling Jesus "Lord." The Greek word for "Lord," *Kyrios*, is the word used instead of Yahweh in the Greek translation of the Old Testament. So when Thomas calls Jesus, "My *Lord* and my God!" or when Paul calls Jesus "Lord," they are not simply using another title for Jesus; they are telling us that Jesus is God. This is why "no one can say 'Jesus is Lord' except in the Holy Spirit," as Paul says in 1 Corinthians 12:3.

Once we start thinking about this, it may be confusing that we say in the First Article, "I believe in one God, the Father Almighty," and in the Second Article, "And in one Lord Jesus Christ." But it may be helpful to review some of the passages in Paul's letters. Paul's usual practice is to say "God" when he is referring to the Father and "Lord" when he is referring to Jesus. He can call Jesus God as well, but in the Creed we are simply following the biblical usage, especially of Paul.

OPENING PRAYER

O Lord Jesus Christ, You willingly took on human flesh and entered this world; You suffered, died, and rose from the dead in order to restore us and Your whole creation. You have sent Your Spirit to us, so that we may confess You as our Lord, who has redeemed us from sin, death, and the devil, so that we may be Your own and live under You in Your kingdom forever. Keep us by the Spirit in Your Body, the church, with the Father, until we experience the fullness of Your divine life. Amen.

Hymn: "Jesus Has Come and Brings Pleasure" (*Lutheran Service Book* 533)

QUESTION 1: What does it mean to say "Jesus is Lord"?

ANSWER 1: The focus is on how saying, "Jesus is Lord," is equivalent to saying, "Jesus is God."

QUESTION 2: Why does the Creed specify that the Son was begotten of the Father "before all worlds"?

ANSWER 2: When we say, "begotten of His Father before all worlds," the Creed literally says "before all ages"—that is, from eternity. When we use the words of the Bible to talk about God, we are always using them by analogy; human words can never quite comprehend the mystery of God. So *beget* is a word used of fathers who have children. But when we are talking about God, it cannot mean what it means to us in normal usage. We confess that the Father begets the Son, but not as human beings do. So essentially we say something that would not make sense according to human use: "eternally begotten." And yet, we confess the mystery.

QUESTION 3: Can you think of other names or titles that are used of both the Father and the Son or of both the Son and the Spirit?

ANSWER 3: "Paraclete" is one (John 14:16). The point goes back to the fourth century, where the defenders of Nicaea argued that if the persons of the Trinity shared the same names, then they must be one being or divine nature.

QUESTION 4: Can you think of other words that are not in the Bible but still say the same thing that the Bible says?

ANSWER 4: I am thinking primarily of the word *Trinity*, which is not in the Bible but still confesses the truth about God. Perhaps participants will be able to think of others.

QUESTION 5: "The Word" in John 1 is the Greek word *Logos*, which had connotations not only of spoken words but also of reason. If Jesus is the Word made flesh, what other, richer sense can it add when we think not only of the Scriptures as the written Word of God but also of whenever God speaks and what His Word accomplishes?

ANSWER 5: You might explore here the nature of God's Word—written, preached, read, heard—in relation to Jesus as *the* Word of God. You could look at the creation, where God speaks and things happen. Isaiah 55:1–13 and Romans 10:14–17 may be helpful as well.

QUESTION 6: What is the opposite of faith? Knowledge or sight? What difference does it make for how we talk about what we believe?

ANSWER 6: Faith is not the opposite of knowledge; it is a different way of knowing. Faith is the opposite of sight, because we must believe not what we do not know but what we do not see. Faith is not a leap into the dark but clinging to a promise made by our faithful God. See also 2 Corinthians 5:7; Hebrews 11:1.

FOR FURTHER INVESTIGATION

Athanasius of Alexandria, *Against the Arians* (you can find a free, online version here: ccel.org)

Gregory of Nazianzus, *Theological Orations*, especially Orations 3 and 4 (also online at ccel.org)

ADDITIONAL INFORMATION

Why did Arius object to describing the Son as eternal with the Father? At least part of the issue, as Arius saw it, was that Alexander's statement sounded to Arius like a heresy called Sabellianism. In the third century (around the year 215), there was a priest named Sabellius—possibly in Rome—who apparently taught that God was absolutely one, so that the Father, Son, and Holy Spirit were three "modes" of God. (This is why another name for this false teaching is Modalism.) Part of the problem between Arius and Alexander was that some of the words used for "person" (*hypostasis*) or "substance/being" (*ousia*) were not yet specific in their meaning, and so people used them in different ways. Arius believed that saying both the Father and the Son were eternal had to mean that they were essentially the same person. He could not see how there could be more than one "eternal." There can only be one "first"!

Eventually, especially because of the work of the Cappadocian theologians (Basil the Great, Gregory of Nazianzus, and Gregory of Nyssa), these words took on specific meaning. This illustrates what often happens in theological controversies: Prior to the controversy, a word might be used more or less loosely, and even in ways that later theologians might judge unorthodox or even heretical. Once the controversy happens, the meaning of certain words becomes more limited. Martin Chemnitz saw this issue in the sixteenth century as well. He cited Augustine: "'When you Pelagians were not yet causing contention, the fathers spoke less carefully about these articles' (*Contra Julianum*, Bk. 1)—that is, outside of contention, when controversies had not yet arisen, the fathers frequently discussed many things not with precision but in a more carefree way. But these less careful statements must not, as Augustine says, be twisted for a protection of things that do not agree with the Scripture."[7]

BONUS QUESTIONS

1. What similarities are there between the controversies in the fourth century and the controversies in the sixteenth century?

2. Can we count the things we believe as knowledge? Is the distinction between what we know and what we believe a false distinction created with the Enlightenment?

3. For now "we walk by faith, not by sight," (2 Corinthians 5:7), but when will that be reversed and we no longer need faith?

---

[7] Martin Chemnitz, *Examination of the Council of Trent, Part 1*, trans. Fred Kramer (Concordia Publishing House, 1971), 261.

Leader Guide for Session 4

For Us

KEY TAKEAWAYS

It is essential to the Christian Gospel that it be *for me, for us*. It must be applied to me, not just a general truth about God. Here, the Creed makes clear what is implicit throughout: All this God has done for us in Christ by the Spirit, without any merit or worthiness in us.

OPENING PRAYER

Almighty God, You have called Your church to witness that in Christ You have reconciled us to Yourself. Grant that by Your Holy Spirit we may proclaim the good news of Your salvation so that all who hear it may receive the gift of salvation; through Jesus Christ, our Lord. Amen.

Hymn: "Glory Be to Jesus" (*Lutheran Service Book* 433)

QUESTION 1: In Acts 4:12, Peter insists that "there is salvation in no one else [than Jesus], for there is no other name under heaven given among men by which we must be saved." How is this both Law and Gospel?

ANSWER 1: In the terms of the Law, Peter's words cut off our own chosen ways of salvation. In terms of the Gospel, God provides for our salvation precisely in Jesus, so that we do not have to go searching, trying to figure out where we might find salvation.

QUESTION 2: How is every true confession about Mary really a confession of Jesus?

ANSWER 2: Mary is often a touchy subject among Lutherans, but it is important not to fall into misunderstandings or false belief, if that belief touches on who Jesus is as God.

QUESTION 3: What does the mention of Pontius Pilate tell us about how God works in the world beyond what we can see?

ANSWER 3: Here, you might discuss how the Bible does not give us a version of history that we compare against the "real" world. Instead, the Bible's story, from creation to consummation, gives us the true story, into which everything else fits.

QUESTION 4: What are two things we can learn from what Jesus, Paul, and Peter say about Jesus' suffering?

Leader Guide for Session 4: For Us

ANSWER 4: Among other things, we learn that Jesus' suffering was divinely necessary. (The little Greek word *dei* means "it is necessary.") Also, we learn that the whole story of the Scriptures leads up to Jesus' suffering and death ("it is written"). There may be other possibilities.

QUESTION 5: Why is "for you" and "for us" so essential to the Gospel?

ANSWER 5: The proclamation of the Gospel emphasizes that the saving Gospel of Jesus is "for you." When we hear that and believe it, we then confess that it is "for us," as in the Creed. You could focus on the repeated "given and shed for you for the forgiveness of sins" in the Small Catechism's explanations to the Sacrament of the Altar. Perhaps discussion might go to the personal, subjective nature of those words "for *you*."

FOR FURTHER INVESTIGATION

Solid Declaration of the Formula of Concord, Article 8: The Person of Christ

J. N. D. Kelly, *Early Christian Creeds*, 3rd ed. (Longman, 1972), especially chapters 10 and 11.

Martin Luther, "On the Councils and the Church," trans. Charles M. Jacobs, ed. Eric W. Gritsch, *Luther's Works,* vol. 41 (Fortress Press, 1966), 3–178.

ADDITIONAL INFORMATION

One kind of false teaching about Jesus, which had been around since the time of the New Testament, was called Docetism. It was the idea that Jesus only "seemed" to be human (the Greek word for "to think/

seem" is *dokeō*). This teaching was officially condemned at the Council of Nicaea, although it had been around for a long time. After Nicaea, a bishop named Nestorius (who strongly defended the Creed of Nicaea), argued against calling Mary *Theotokos* ("God-bearer"). Even though Nestorius believed that Jesus had both a human and a divine nature, he thought it was inappropriate to call Mary the "mother of God." At the Council of Chalcedon in 451, Cyril of Alexandria (among others) had Nestorius condemned. To say that Mary is the mother of God is not mainly saying something about Mary but something about Jesus: that He was and is God. The Lutheran Confessions affirm the judgment of Cyril and the Council of Chalcedon in the Formula of Concord (Epitome, Article 8, paragraph 7, and Solid Declaration, Article 8, paragraph 24).

In the sixteenth century, argument over the Lord's Supper and the presence of Christ's body and blood being eaten and drunk was connected to Jesus' two natures (divine and human, in one person). The Reformed position was that Jesus' human body had to remain in heaven, even if Jesus made Himself spiritually present to us in the Supper or if we ascended spiritually to commune with Jesus' body and blood in heaven. The Lutherans argued that for Jesus to be Jesus, He must be, at all times, that one person with both a divine and a human nature. Thus, when He comes to us in the Sacrament, it must be with both His divine nature and His true body and blood, or else it is no longer the same Jesus.

BONUS QUESTIONS

1. What are the implications of Jesus' earthly life and death if He did not have a truly human body?

2. What are the implications today if He does not now have His human body, though glorified?

3. What are the implications for our resurrection bodies in light of Jesus' resurrection body?

Leader Guide for Session 5

The Everlasting King

KEY TAKEAWAYS

Here we confess the exaltation and glorification of the Son of God in flesh, after His suffering and death. The Gospel theme continues, as we connect what Jesus has done with the "for you" of our own resurrection and sharing in His glory before the Father. These are not only essential elements of the Christian Faith, but they recount the story of God's salvation for us.

OPENING PRAYER

Almighty God, our heavenly Father, because of Your tender love toward us sinners You have given us Your Son that, believing in Him, we might have everlasting life. Continue to grant us Your Holy Spirit that we may remain steadfast in this faith to the end and finally come to life everlasting; through Jesus Christ, our Lord. Amen.

Hymn: "Jesus Lives! The Victory's Won" (*Lutheran Service Book* 490)

QUESTION 1: What are "the Scriptures" according to which Jesus rose from the dead?

ANSWER 1: Here is an opportunity to explore the fact that the "Scriptures" of which Paul speaks are what we call the Old Testament. Thus, the entire story of the Old Testament is fulfilled in Jesus' death and resurrection. This is not what is "new" about the New Testament.

QUESTION 2: How would you describe the importance of the ascension to someone?

ANSWER 2: Here you might consider John 14:12 and how Jesus' works will be spread far and wide throughout the church because of His ascension, rather than being located exactly where He is on the earth during His earthly lifetime.

QUESTION 3: From these verses or others, what activity does the right hand of God represent or include?

ANSWER 3: The answers are many: God's power, salvation, deliverance, ruling, judgment, and so on.

QUESTION 4: From these passages (or others), how would you describe the judgment of God, in contrast to how most people think of God's judging?

Leader Guide for Session 5: The Everlasting King

ANSWER 4: The emphasis here is that the judgment of God is in Christ and not simply at some time in the future. *Judgment*, in itself, is a neutral word. It means condemnation only as ongoing unbelief in Jesus, who has appeared in the world. But to those who believe Jesus, judgment means salvation and resurrection, which is why God sent Jesus into the world. Outside of individual believers or unbelievers, it also means the restoration of all things in God's creation, as all evil is removed. Christians rejoice with the whole creation (see Psalm 98 and Romans 8) at the judgment of God that falls on them for Christ's sake because it means Christ's righteousness instead of their unrighteousness.

QUESTION 5: John and Jesus both say that the "kingdom of heaven is at hand" or "has come near." What are the signs that Jesus does to show that His kingdom has come on earth?

ANSWER 5: Everything Jesus does shows that God's gracious reign and rule have come on the earth in Him. For example, He turns water into far more wine than the people need or probably even can drink (see John 2:1–12)! And He feeds more than five thousand people with a little bread and fish (see John 6:1–14) and has more left over! With such miracles, He demonstrates an end to the lack that characterizes our life in this world. Further, He casts out demons (which will happen completely on the Last Day) and He heals the sick and raises the dead (which will happen universally on the Last Day).

QUESTION 6: How does the confession of Jesus' resurrection, ascension, glorification at the right hand of the Father and His future return in glory give us assurance and hope for our lives here and now?

ANSWER 6: This is how the Gospel produces fruit in our lives and confident, loving service of our neighbor. We do not do good works in order to earn anything, but out of the assurance of God's salvation in Christ, we are freed to do what our neighbor requires of us—even as we continually return to Christ's Word and Sacraments, which are the source and sustenance of our new and eternal life.

FOR FURTHER INVESTIGATION

Solid Declaration of the Formula of Concord, Article 7: The Holy Supper

Large Catechism, Part 3, paragraphs 49–58

ADDITIONAL INFORMATION

In the sixteenth century, the ascension became a point of contention—not over whether it happened but what it meant for Jesus' presence with us, especially with regard to the Sacrament of the Altar. The Reformed contended that Jesus' ascension meant that His body, because it was a real human body, could only be present in one place at one time. Therefore, in order for us to commune with Jesus' body and blood, we must be ascending spiritually to commune with Jesus in heaven. The Lutherans, on the other hand, confessed that the ascension and glorification of Jesus in His body means that He exercises His divine power in and with His human body. Although it is not proper to a human body to be present in more than one place, it is proper to God, and therefore to Jesus' divine nature. Since He is one person, if Jesus is present with us at all, He must be present as both God and man. When He says, "take and eat, this is My body" or "take and drink, this cup is the new testament in My blood," we are not communing only with His divine nature but with the whole Jesus—divine and human. Thus, the ascension becomes the basis for our assurance of Jesus' true and entire presence with us, just as He said.

There are many, many passages about God's "right hand" in the Scriptures, encompassing His salvation, preservation, provision, and protection of His people. Meditation on all those passages could be a whole study in itself. You might encourage people to take up that study in their personal devotional reading.

BONUS QUESTION

1. How does the confession that Christ's kingdom will not come to an end give us confidence?

Leader Guide for Session 6
The Lord and Giver of Life

KEY TAKEAWAYS

This session covers the post-Nicene controversies around the confession of the Holy Spirit as equally God with the Father and the Son. The same titles and names are used of the Spirit as are used of the Father and the Son. And we believe in the Spirit not only as an abstract member of the Godhead but as the Spirit who is given in the world to call, create, and grow the church of God in Jesus Christ.

OPENING PRAYER

O God, on this day You once taught the hearts of Your faithful people by sending them the light of Your Holy Spirit. Grant us in our day the same Spirit to have a right understanding in all things and evermore to rejoice in His holy consolation; through Jesus Christ, Your Son, our Lord, who lives and reigns with You and the Holy Spirit, one God, now and forever. Amen.

Hymn: "Come, Holy Ghost, God and Lord" (*Lutheran Service Book* 497)

QUESTION 1: What in these passages (or others) shows that the Holy Spirit is a distinct person of the Trinity but neither another God nor a creature of God?

ANSWER 1: This is the constant danger that people faced in the fourth century (and that we still face): to avoid emphasizing "one God" so that we lose the distinction of Father, Son, and Holy Spirit and to avoid emphasizing the three persons so that we lose the unity of God.

QUESTION 2: How does the Spirit give life?

ANSWER 2: Here, emphasis is on the specific, concrete means that God uses to give us life. It is not purely "spiritual" in the sense that most people use that word. In John 3:5–6, Jesus tells Nicodemus (and us) that the Spirit gives new, spiritual life by the water of Holy Baptism. The Spirit gives life by the Word in and through those who speak that Word according to their vocations. The Spirit gives life by opening ears and hearts to that Word, so that people believe Jesus, who says that His flesh is given for the life of the world (see John 6:33, 51).

QUESTION 3: How would you describe the procession of the Spirit according to the above passages (or others)?

ANSWER 3: The Spirit is fully God, sent by the Father and given by the Son, in the one will of the Holy Trinity.

QUESTION 4: Where in the liturgies of the church do you see this worship of Father, Son, and Spirit?

ANSWER 4: Here is an opportunity to explore the liturgy in its trinitarian dimension (e.g., the Invocation, Absolution, and Benediction).

QUESTION 5: From these passages (or others), how would you describe the Holy Spirit speaking "by the prophets"?

ANSWER 5: We want to confess that no Scripture comes to us except by the Holy Spirit, but the Spirit uses many ways to get that Word to the prophets, and so to us. The specific methods of the Spirit are not always easy to nail down. And yet we can be confident that we have the Scriptures exactly as the Spirit wants us to have them.

QUESTION 6: Consider Exodus 34:5–8. How is God's name more than just what He is called?

ANSWER 6: You might consider the Small Catechism's explanation of the First Petition of the Lord's Prayer and how the *name of God is what He does*. So when God's name is put on us, that is an active, forgiving, saving work.

FOR FURTHER INVESTIGATION

J. N. D. Kelly, *Early Christian Creeds*, 3rd ed. (Longman, 1972), especially pages 338–44 and 358–67.

Large Catechism, Part 2, paragraphs 34–70

David R. Maxwell, "The Nicene Creed in the Church," *Concordia Journal* 41:1 (2015): 16–20.

ADDITIONAL INFORMATION

The confession that the Spirit proceeds from the Father and the Son goes back to various creeds of the fourth and fifth centuries. Probably it first appeared in the Niceno-Constantinopolitan Creed in Spain around the end of the sixth century. As often happens, this division became hardened in the eighth century, and it is still a contentious point of division between East and West.[8]

BONUS QUESTIONS

1. Even though Lutherans spend a lot of time in the Second Article, how is the Third Article essential to believing Jesus?

2. How do John 14:25–27; 15:26–27; and 16:12–15 open up for you new ways of thinking about the Spirit with the Father and the Son and the trinitarian work of salvation and sanctification in the church?

---

8 Kelly, *Early Christian Creeds*, 363–67

Leader Guide for Session 7
The Temple of the Holy Spirit

KEY TAKEAWAYS

The previous session focused on the person of the Holy Spirit. Here, we are focused on the Holy Spirit's work of creating, nourishing, sustaining, perfecting, and making holy the church. The adjectives that describe the church (*one*, *holy*, *Christian*, and *apostolic*) come from the Scriptures, and this is a confession of faith, not of what we can see. The Holy Spirit's work in and for the church, especially via Holy Baptism, comes to its fulfillment and completion in the "resurrection of the dead and the life of the world to come."

OPENING PRAYER

Almighty God, grant to Your church Your Holy Spirit and the wisdom that comes down from above, that Your Word may not be bound but have free course and be preached to the joy and edifying of Christ's holy people, that in steadfast faith we may serve You and, in the confession of Your name, abide unto the end; through Jesus Christ, our Lord. Amen.

Hymn: "Holy Spirit, Ever Dwelling" (*Lutheran Service Book* 650)

QUESTION 1: Though we put the church under the Third Article of the Creed (the Holy Spirit), how is the church a trinitarian creation?

ANSWER 1: We should always remember that even though we associate certain things with the Father, or the Son, or the Spirit, the persons of the Trinity are never active apart from each other. Creation is trinitarian, redemption is trinitarian (though the incarnation belongs to the Son alone), and sanctification in the church is trinitarian.

QUESTION 2: How is Baptism like birth and also like death?

ANSWER 2: Here is an opportunity to open up the range of images connected with Baptism: new birth of the new creature in Christ, death of the old creature in Adam. You could show images of different kinds of ancient baptismal fonts (easily searchable on the internet; look for crosses, graves, wombs, etc.).

QUESTION 3: How would you describe the importance of the resurrection to the Christian life?

ANSWER 3: There is no overstating of the importance of the resurrection, but we may not have thought about the implications since we are so familiar with the idea of "dying and going to heaven." Here is an opportunity to explore the fullness of our confession. What implications are there for how we (mis)use our bodies? What implications are there for Christians' funerals and burial practices?

QUESTION 4: How would you respond to someone who warns against being so heavenly minded that we are of no earthly good? Or someone who says that we should be more concerned about the good we're doing on earth than about where we go when we die? Or the person who says that we do not need to worry about creation here and now because it is all going to be destroyed?

ANSWER 4: The idea here is not to denigrate the coming fulfillment of God's promise in Christ, in resurrection and new creation, but also not to denigrate the creation and our bodies here and now. God created humans as both body and soul to live in this world, and it is as body-and-soul people that He will raise us from the dead to live in the new earth under new heavens.

QUESTION 5: If you were asked how people should recognize the true church, since there are so many denominations with competing claims, how would you answer?

ANSWER 5: Here is an opportunity to explore the meaning of "marks of the church."

FOR FURTHER INVESTIGATION

Large Catechism, Part 4

Augsburg Confession, Articles 5, 7, 8, 13–17

Regin Prenter, *Spiritus Creator* (Fortress Press, 1953; repr., Wipf and Stock, 2001).

ADDITIONAL INFORMATION

From the book of Acts, we know that the church and the Holy Spirit are intimately connected. One of the areas where you might spend more time is on each of the adjectives in this second part of the Third Article. Starting with the passages from Ephesians in the first section, it may be helpful to unpack "one," "holy," "Christian/catholic," and "apostolic." It may also help to clarify the true sense of "catholic." This word means "according to the whole," or "universal." There is also an opportunity here to focus on the ultimate hope of the Christian faith and life, which is not simply dying and going to heaven (although Paul says that would be better than remaining in a sinful body in a sinful world) but the resurrection of the dead and the life everlasting. We confess that our bodies will be raised from the dead, not that we will live in the clouds only as souls or as angels. God made human beings as body and soul, and we wait for the day when we will again be body and soul, though without sin and death. (Jesus' own resurrected human body is the key image here.)

BONUS QUESTIONS

1. Why does it matter that Lutherans are catholic (though not Roman Catholic, of course)? If we consider ourselves less than the universal church, why is that a problem for our understanding of the church? If we concede to the Church of Rome the title "catholic," as the universal church, what does that make Lutherans?

2. Why does it matter that we confess the resurrection of the body, rather than just the separation of the body and soul at death? How do we know that our bodies, along with the rest of the physical creation, are important to God?

Leader Guide for Session 8
The Story Becomes Our Story

KEY TAKEAWAYS

To finish up our study, we want to connect the story told in the Scriptures, for which the Creed supplies an essential outline, to the story that we each tell of our own lives.

OPENING PRAYER

Almighty God, send Your Holy Spirit into our hearts that He may rule and direct us according to Your will, comfort us in all our temptations and afflictions, defend us from all error, and lead us into all truth that we, being steadfast in faith, may increase in all good works and in the end obtain everlasting life. Amen.

Hymn: "O God, My Faithful God" (*Lutheran Service Book* 696)

QUESTION 1: Whose story is primary, ours or God's? If asked, Christians will likely say God's, but how does that work out in practice in our lives? What difference does it make for your life if you think of the Bible's story as the story into which you are written at Baptism rather than thinking of your story as the main story into which God and the Bible have to fit?

ANSWER 1: For example, if God's story is the story into which our stories are written, this relieves us of the anxiety of self-creation, of trying to make ourselves into something in this world. It is a comfort for us to know that God has written the story all the way to the end, and Jesus' life, death, and resurrection are the basic outline of that story. What happened to Jesus will happen to us, since we are members of His Body.

QUESTION 2: How would you explain to someone why we continue to use these ancient words each Sunday?

ANSWER 2: If we really want to get to know another person, we listen to and learn the stories that that person tells about him- or herself. If we want people to get to know us, we tell them stories about our lives. God has told us a story so that we will know Him. It is the story of God's creation, redemption, and sanctification, centered in the flesh and blood of Jesus. This is the story we hear and confess in the Creed(s), but it is also the story that is told in an orderly way throughout the year in the liturgy of the church. We hear different parts of that story, from the promise of Christ's return in glory to His birth to His revelation as Savior of the world to His suffering, death, resurrection, ascension, and sending of the Holy Spirit. But then we also move into the second half of the Church Year, where the story of Jesus' life forms and shapes our lives as we are remade in the image of Jesus, who is the image of God.

FOR FURTHER INVESTIGATION

J. N. D. Kelly, *Early Christian Creeds*, 3rd ed. (Longman, 1972).

Edward Yarnold, S. J., *Cyril of Jerusalem* (Routledge, 2000).

ADDITIONAL INFORMATION

We often think of our own lives as a story. We think of our beginning at birth and our ending at death, and we tell that story with the events and people we consider important. The closer we get to the end of the story, the better picture we have of how things fit together, as we have made choices and followed certain paths. This is *our* story, and we decide what fits and how it fits. The things that might fit include God, Jesus, the Scriptures, attendance at the Divine Service, and how and what we teach our children. But is our story primary?

The Creed teaches, shapes, and forms us (along with the rest of the Scriptures and the regular gathering of the Lord's people on the Lord's Day for the Divine Service) to think of God's story as primary. Our story is only one tiny subplot of God's story of salvation. But we have been put into and joined to the living Word of that story in Jesus. Now, instead of struggling to see whether and how God fits into our story, we have the comforting assurance that we—who have been made by God, redeemed by Jesus, and gathered to Christ by the Holy Spirit—have been incorporated into a story of which we already know the ending in Jesus. *The story has become our story.*

BONUS QUESTION

It may be helpful to read aloud some of Cyril's catechetical sermons and imagine what it must have been like for those catechumens. Catechesis 10 has one part where he points to the place of Jesus' death and of His resurrection, saying that the fragments of the cross are "still to be seen among us today," that Golgotha "rises above us here," and that the grave of Jesus is "still lying there."[9]

The beginning of Edward Yarnold's book on Cyril of Jerusalem also has a section on Egeria, a fourth-century pilgrim to Jerusalem, who wrote down much of what she saw. She gives us a firsthand account of the way that things happened in Jerusalem.

For both Cyril and Egeria, there was only a very little distance between the events of Jesus' life and the life of Christians.

1. What are some ways we might recover some of what they experienced, though we cannot go back to their time?

---

9 Edward Yarnold, S. J., *Cyril of Jerusalem*, The Early Church Fathers (Routledge, 2000), 127. Reproduced by permission of Taylor & Francis Group.